W0007637

Written by Sally A Jones and Amanda C Jones
Front Cover Photo by Annalisa Jones
USA Editing: S. Waller

Published by GUINEA PIG EDUCATION

2 Cobs Way,
New Haw,
Addlestone,
Surrey,
KT15 3AF.
www.guineapigeducation.co.uk

ISBN: 978-1-907733-87-1

Noah

Hi Kids,

These are the books you've been waiting for to help you with your writing assignments, especially if you're preparing for an exam.

There are three books in total. This one helps you to practice persuasive writing for your classes and also for standardized exams. Use it in different ways. Read the pieces of writing over and over again. Complete the exercises. Cover the writing and try to rewrite them in your own style in paragraphs. You will learn to develop your main points, give evidence and make explanations.

Have fun writing!

When you _write_ to persuade

Ask yourself:

Have I managed to get him or her to see my point of view?

When you write to persuade you need to convince your reader to believe in your point of view. It is important that you write in an interesting way, in a clear style, so you must organize your thoughts.

You want your reader to keep reading and to be able to recall what they read, so you must use the right words.

Persuade people to visit:

A new 'Seaside World' has recently been built to give people the chance to discover more about endangered species. A lot of money has been spent building the center and the work carried out is crucial for the survival of many sea creatures.

However, due to bad weather during the summer, fewer people have visited the center than expected. It has not covered its costs and if it has to close many animals will lose their homes.

The owners are very worried. <u>They have asked you to produce a leaflet to persuade people to visit the center.</u>

What you write is **very important.** It is up to you to save the center.

In your leaflet you could answer the following questions that people will ask:

- *Why should I visit the center?*
- *What is there for me to see and do?*
- *Include any additional information, such as costs and opening times*

A plan to *persuade* people to visit 'Seaside World'...

VISIT	our cafe selling hot and cold drinks, delicious snacks and ice creams.
EXPLORE	our shop selling souvenirs, postcards, pencils, pens, erasers and books.
JOIN US	on our daily boat trips, which take you out to sea.
DISCOVER	the fascinating world that exists under the water, from the safety of our glass-bottomed boat.
ENJOY	a few hours diving or hire your own boat on our large lake.
RELAX	by our peaceful lake for an afternoon of fishing. We can provide you with all equipment needed.
TAKE	the opportunity to swim with dolphins! Watch our show where you will learn all you ever wanted to know about this amazing creature.
MARVEL	at the range of colorful and exotic fish in our aquarium.
SELECT	one of our educational DVD's, to learn about the problems facing endangered species.

Remember:
BOSSY VERBS - like 'Take' and 'Relax' are imperatives and instruct people to do things.

Now, it is your turn:

Come to 'Seaside World' and have fun finding out about endangered species. The whole family is welcome. Teachers can bring their classes so the children can learn how to help the animals. It will be a fantastic day out for everyone.

If you take one of our boat trips you will... *exotic fish and you may even see a shark*

In the tropical aquarium .... *you will see alligators and*

When you watch the whale exhibition DVD you will ... *see and hear whales communicating with other whales.*

Parents with young children must visit... *the play centers to see and touch at the dolphins.*

When you feel thirsty you can get yourself a drink at ... *the snack stand. You can also get a yummy snack.*

It only costs ... *$1.00 + tax.*

You will find us at ... *1234 Main Street Chicago, Il.*

The times of opening are ... *from 12pm - 1am.*

SEE YOU SOON

6

If you want a taste of mountain life come to *Chamonix* in the *French Alps*...

You can rent this beautiful chalet with stunning views across the mountains. It can be discovered in a woodland valley on the peaceful alpine slopes surrounded by animals grazing, where you will hear the cowbells jingling.

The chalet has pretty baskets of flowers on the wooden balconies and shutters at the windows to block out bad weather. Inside, it has comfortable furniture in a traditional mountain style. It has all the equipment you need, including a microwave, a dishwasher and

cooking utensils. Children can amuse themselves on play equipment or befriend the donkey. The whole family will have fun walking through the mountain slopes or visiting the craft shops where they can buy souvenirs.

If you take a walk or drive you will see snowy mountain peaks or even an amazing glacier. You can ride to the top of the mountains by cable car. Then you can drive to the many medieval towns and villages nearby and even treat yourself to a pizza at a local restaurant.

The chalet is for up to 6 people. It has four rooms: two singles, one double and one with bunk beds. The cost is $800 per week or $1400 for two weeks.

This amazing resort will make you feel that you never want to go home!

Imagine your dream travel destination: maybe a tropical island or busy city.
Persuade others to go there:

1. Start by writing sentences for an introduction. Begin with one of the following:

   - *If you want a taste of .... come to ....*
   - *You will never be bored at ....*
   - *There is something for the whole family at ....*

2. Describe the accommodation (villa, chalet or apartment) in three sentences. Use good adjectives (descriptive words) with your nouns:

   - *comfortable bed*
   - *pretty garden*
   - *stunning sea views and breathtaking scenery*
   - *scorching sun*

3. Use good adverbs with your verbs:

   - *The sun always shines brightly.*

4. Next include a further paragraph explaining what children can do here and what the family can see, do and experience.

5. Continue by writing another paragraph of useful information, like:

   - *the costs*
   - *size of accommodation*
   - *how to get to your chosen travel destination*

6. Finally, conclude by writing a catchy ending:

   - *You'll never want to go home!*
   - *A vacation with us is a once in a lifetime experience!*
   - *Don't miss out. Book today!*

Appeal to parents. They are your target audience.

Does your child long for adventure?

Come to LANDSCOMBE
Adventure Park

A vacation with us is an exciting and challenging experience that your child will never forget.

An adventure vacation at Landscombe offers your child the chance to take part in a range of supervised activities and sports, including rock climbing, walking, swimming, canoeing, sailing, horse riding and even wind surfing. It is an opportunity for your child to learn new skills, make new friends and improve their fitness.

Our center is set on a 30-acre estate in the countryside near the sea. The children will be organized into groups to participate in their chosen activities. All our instructors are qualified teachers, who are trained in first aid, so you can be sure your child is in safe hands.

(Think about whom you are trying to persuade. Parents like to know about safety.)

Whether your child chooses to learn tennis on one of our tennis courts or prefers to have swimming lessons in the heated pool, he or she will have a fantastic time.

Your child will have his or her own room. All rooms include their own bathroom, a satellite television and stunning sea views.

Have You Heard Enough?

I think you'll agree this is an opportunity too good to miss.

For just $850 per week your child could enjoy our vacation as countless other children have.

Book NOW to avoid disappointment.

1. Write down in a sentence what the vacation offers.

   *sports
   * individual rooms w/ bathrooms
   * supervised activity

2. Write down in a sentence what facilities the center offers.

3. Find four opportunities your child would have on the vacation listed in the text.

   * about wildlife
   * how to play sports
   * friendships

4. Draw a box with necessary information, details of cost etc.

Remember:
Address your reader directly using 'you' and 'your child.'

Complete, filling in the missing information:

RUSHFORD TOURS

Come and enjoy the historic sights of Rushford on the City Sight ....
...Tours..... with departures at ....4pm.............. On our hop on-hop off double-decker bus you can climb aboard at ......the....... capital building...

Our fully open top buses ensure that you have a spectacular view of Rushford so you.....sit back and relax............ and enjoy the ride..

All our younger passengers get .....free candy, and.... a bobble head batman or...... batgirl.................................

The tour has an experienced guide who tells you .....fun facts... about the city as well as...... the arcteurture of the building....

When you've experienced the amazing sights of Rushford from our bus you can visit ....the capital building and.. museums.................... to buy ...merchandise...... .... or eat out at .....Calcynous Restaurants where you will enjoy the most delicious .....sushi w/ wasab.

The cost of the tour is only ....$100 per family......

Don't miss the opportunity to .....experience this... wonderful tour........................

We look forward to seeing you SOON!

Persuade families to visit:

THE COUNTRYWISE RARE BREEDS CENTER

Our rare breeds center is a very special place that is well worth a visit. You will fall in love with our friendly animals. There is an opportunity to get right up close to them in the petting zoo. Bring the whole family for a fun day out. Take a turn helping at feeding time.

This is a place where you can really get involved and learn lots of information as well.

You will be able to enter the pen of our unusual spotty breed of bull. He is so tame you can stroke him and he will lick your hand. There is also an opportunity to feed the newborn lambs from the bottle. Come aboard the badger train, which takes you deep into the heart of the Wild Wood. Here you may catch a glimpse of Mrs. Badger coming out of her sett to forage for food for the cubs. School children can visit The Countrywise Museum and fill in the fun fact sheet.

Of course, don't forget to bring some money for the souvenir shop.

If you get hungry visit the .... Pasta center. There are different kinds of pasta with 10 delectable sauces. For dessert go and get Leo's Ice cream.

There are also laser tag animal games for kids it is fun for all ages.

.... and an adventure playground. You will be so glad you came.

We look forward to seeing you.

There is nowhere like it!

It is totally unique.

It is amazing.

A fun, family day out.

Remember: short sentences are convincing.

'You' is second person and will get the attention of your reader.

Write your own leaflet persuading people to visit. Draw a map or picture.

Pinewood Gardens

If you love to relax in beautiful countryside, surrounded by pretty gardens, you will enjoy a visit to Pinewood. It has a thousand different kinds of trees, including some rare ones. In the spring it has some of the most impressive displays of bluebells in the country and trees covered with blossoms. The autumn leaves have stunning colors. Whatever time of year you visit, you will find it a very peaceful place.

Why not join one of our guided tours to learn about birds and wildlife? Take a walk around the lake and stop at the boathouse, which has a viewing gallery, where you can watch different species of birds in their habitats. There is always an abundance of wildlife to see. You are welcome to bring your dog, but keep him on a leash. Before you go home, visit our cozy tea shop located on the edge of the woods, which sells the most delicious homemade cakes.

The park is open every day, from eleven to five. You will find us near the forest .... off the Coust off Massachutes MA

The cost is $59.99

Make a day of it!

Persuade your reader to visit. List all the things he or she can do. Read, cover and write your own version.

CLARE HOUSE

Clare House is a delightful fifteenth century mansion, surrounded by the rolling hills of the English countryside. The house has been

restored to its original appearance, as it would have looked in Tudor times. You can take a step back in time as you wander through the historic rooms, with their fine furnishings, which include servants' quarters and a working kitchen with blazing log fires. Look out for the secret passage concealed behind a bookcase. There is a priceless collection of paintings by famous artists and the gardens are also delightful to walk in.

Whatever age you are, there is plenty to do here. We promise you will never be bored. Gardeners will find lots of tips and free advice in the gardens. There are nature trails on the grounds for the whole family. School children can participate in the discovery weeks, learning about history by dressing up in period costume and taking part in a Tudor banquet. In addition to this, children's week offers lots of fun, with activities, such as mazes, facts sheets and competitions.

To remember your visit, there are a selection of souvenirs you can buy in our extensive gift shop. You can relax on the lawn with a picnic or visit our coffee shop which sells delicious coffee and teas.

The house and gardens are open every day, from..9.t.0.... .....9.p.m........ to .... The cost is only £.5.9.9.9.... You will find us at ..F.t.i.l.X.j.R.h. ....

A visit to Clare House is always a treat.

Vary sizes of print so important information is large.

Words with the same sound use alliteration.

The tone is the voice the writer speaks in. It is the attitude of the writer that will influence the reader.

Use pronouns like 'you' to make the reader feel the writer is talking to them.

Write from an impersonal point of view using third person (he or they).

Use headings and subheadings.

Use present tense.

Writing to **persuade** in
leaflets, advertisements and brochures.

Aim to sell.

Use persuasive language.

Use slogans, captions and catchphrases that stick in your mind.

Use a formal style with technical or scientific words or use an informal, friendly style.

Structure your work to keep the reader's interest.

Use emotive words to make the reader feel – happy, sad or concerned.

Write from a personal point of view using 1 st person (I, my, us, we) or using second person (you, yours) to grab the attention of your reader.

Presentation is the way the information is set out on the page or screen.

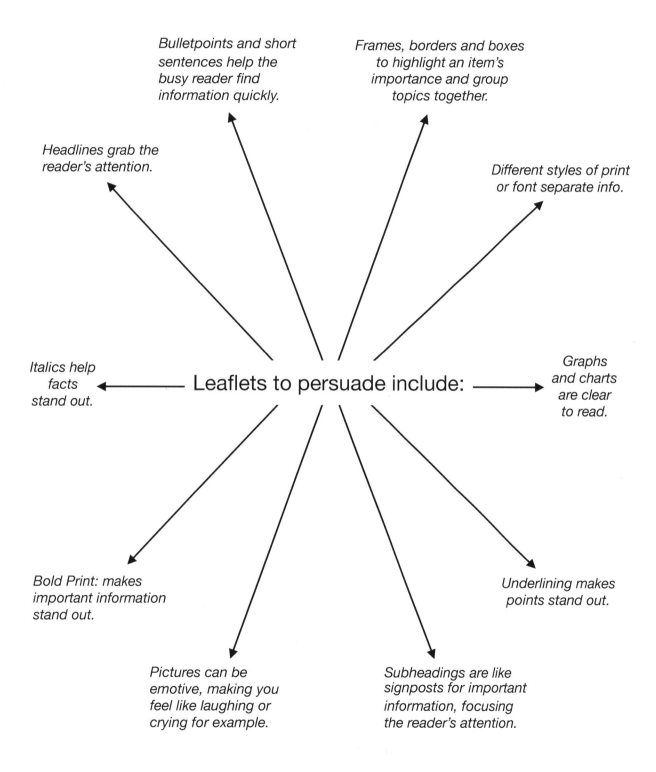

Bulletpoints and short sentences help the busy reader find information quickly.

Frames, borders and boxes to highlight an item's importance and group topics together.

Headlines grab the reader's attention.

Different styles of print or font separate info.

Italics help facts stand out.

Leaflets to persuade include:

Graphs and charts are clear to read.

Bold Print: makes important information stand out.

Underlining makes points stand out.

Pictures can be emotive, making you feel like laughing or crying for example.

Subheadings are like signposts for important information, focusing the reader's attention.

Shock your reader by using _emotive words_.

Finish the information leaflet.

Writing to persuade in an _advertisement_.

Now it is your turn to write an advertisement persuading people to buy a product of your choice. It could be a new chocolate bar, candy, a new D.V.D., a CD, a pair of sneakers or a vacation.

Remember, your writing should be:

PERSUASIVE
CONVINCING
APPEALING

1. Think about your target audience: the people who will want to read it.

   They could be teenagers, children, parents, and people with a similar lifestyle or the same interests.

2. What is the purpose of your writing?

   To make them buy, of course.

3. Where will it be placed?

   In a magazine perhaps.

4. What does it promise?

   To be better than anything that has come before.

5. Who recommends it?

   The writer speaks with authority, like he knows he's right – so the reader will believe.

6. Have you used scientific language or emotive words?

   like full of essential vitamins

7. Is it aimed at people with a similar lifestyle or who share an interest?

Writing to persuade in *newspapers*.

WATCH OUT!

IS WHAT YOU READ IN NEWSPAPER REPORTS REALLY TRUE?

- They may contain facts.

- They may contain facts mixed with the writer's opinion.

- They may be biased, trying to convince you that the reporter's view is right. For example, editorials have more opinions than facts.

Remember:
Newspapers can be formal (New York Times) and informal (a tabloid). They use third person (he, they, it).

Fact or Fiction?

Strange Sighting Over Rushford

Mr. Jones, a forty-year-old man who works as an electrician, saw an ominous unidentified flying object in the sky over his house on Flower Drive, Rushford on Thursday night.

"I was putting the cat out when I heard a whirring sound. I looked up and there was a green object in the sky, circling around. It was preparing to land in the field at the back of my house. I peered through the fence and watched three aliens get out. They took some plant samples and a sheep. They returned to their space craft and took off."

Miss Evans who lives in a cottage further down the street said, "I also saw a strange object in the sky on Thursday night. I thought it was one of those remote control model aircraft that someone was flying." If you have any further information on these sightings please call the newspaper.

Fiction

21

THE DAILY NEWS

www.thedailynews.com   Reporting local life since 1937   March 22, 2020

EXCLUSIVE: PUPPY FOUND. GOOD HOME NEEDED. CAN ANYONE HELP? *(headline)*

INTERVIEW WITH LOCAL ASPCA OFFICER ABOUT THE IMPORTANCE OF DOGS WEARING COLLARS.

Can you give a home to this dog?
(heading)

This cute little pup needs a new owner...
(subheading)

BY ANYA SMITH

On Friday at 4pm the owners of the Fairview Hotel had a shock when an unexpected guest arrived. He was a King Cavalier pup about 9 months old.

The hotel manager Ken Barker said, "He wandered in and put his paw on the desk as if he was another guest. He looked at us with big black appealing eyes as if he was asking for a room. He is an adorable dog and my staff fell in love with him. They have doted on him."

The hotel receptionist Miss Kind added, "He is so affectionate. He will make a fantastic pet for somebody. I would have had him myself if I had a bigger apartment with a yard."

(illustration)

CAPTION: CAVALIER PUPPY

The dog had been living as a stray in the park and was starving. We are searching for a suitable new owner. An animal with such a gentle nature deserves a good home.

If you love dogs and feel you can help, please call 555-4567.

Quotations and direct speech give the writer a chance to put forward different viewpoints. Indirect or reported speech is also used:

(pull quote)

"Ken Barker said that he wandered in and put his paw on the desk."

Are you persuaded? Would you ask your mom to call this number? Write a reply.

THE DAILY NEWS

www.thedailynews.com   Reporting local life since 1937   August 5, 2020

ONE HUNDRED FACTS YOU DID NOT KNOW ABOUT THE WHITE TIGER.

RESIDENTS OUTRAGED BY PLANS TO MOVE TIGER INTO YARD.

TIGER MAN OF RUSHFORD

NEIGHBORS PETRIFIED OF NEW PLAN FOR TIGER TO MOVE IN.

BY ANYA SMITH

Mr. Jones of Rushford plans to keep a white tiger in his backyard *(fact)*. He has already been working hard building the cages *(opinion in a fact)*.

However, the local people are showing mixed feelings, some being furious with the plans.

Mr. Smith from the city council commented, "I think it will be great. There is no danger to the public. All the cages have been checked professionally."

In contrast, Mrs. Vice spoke out, "I am furious. How can they let anyone keep a dangerous wild animal in their backyard? It's ridiculous." *(opinion)*

Mr. Jones assures us that his animals are completely safe. He says, "I have been involved in many conservation projects and this is very

CAPTION:

important to me. I am saving a rare breed of tiger, which is in danger in its natural habitat."

It seems that Mr. Jones is being very reasonable *(opinion)*. He is protecting one of the planet's most loveable creatures in his home zoo. We should support this work. Is this too much to ask to save the tigers? *(rhetorical)*

23

Write a letter to the newspaper reporter who supports Mr. Jones keeping a tiger in his backyard. Persuade her it is dangerous to keep wild animals in a yard. Get her to sympathize with your point of view.

Acorn Close,
South Rushford.

Rushford Gazette,
Rushford High Street,
Rushford.

Dear Ms. Smith

        A few weeks ago I read your newspaper article about Tod Jones, a man in Rushford who kept a tiger in his backyard. He assured the public that his animal was safe and your article supported his home zoo. I think you will probably change your mind when you hear what happened to me.

I was walking along Rushford High Street when I saw a large white cat. It was too big for an ordinary cat, with large paws and a mouth full of sharp teeth.

As it got closer I realized to my horror that it was a tiger. I couldn't believe my eyes. It was early in the morning so there was no help nearby. Most people were still tucked into their beds and were not aware that a tiger was on the loose.

At this point I remembered the article about Tod Jones, who had permission to keep a tiger in a cage in his backyard. It occurred to me that it had probably escaped. If it was hungry, I was in big trouble.

I slowly took a step back, then another and another (vary the pace to build up tension). I stumbled, falling flat on my back. It was advancing on me, getting closer and closer. Then it heard a whistle; it turned and ran home.

Mr. Jones's animal had escaped, just as everyone feared it would. His tiger had given me such a fright. I could easily have had a heart attack, if the owner's head hadn't appeared over the wall and whistled his pet to come in. I was still shaking with fear when I arrived at the office.

It is totally irresponsible to let wild animals roam loose in the street. Mr. Jones should have his license taken away, before his tiger bites somebody.

Mr. Jones can carry on his 'tiger conservation work' from a refuge for wild cats. I'm sure the local community would raise money for this worthy cause – if only to keep the neighborhood safe.

In my view, keeping a tiger in the backyard of a suburb is preposterous.

Yours sincerely,
Owen

Remember:

- Newspapers can be tabloid (*The Post*) or broadsheet (*The New York Times*).

- They can be informal or formal.

- Newspapers have headlines, subheadings and captions.

- They present facts and opinions.

- They use dialogue to help the reader see a story from different points of view.

<u>Newspapers can be biased:</u>

- The end sentence persuades the reader to take a view for or against.

- They use 3rd person (it, he, they).

- They use direct speech to make the news item exciting and fast moving:

> *Mr. Jones explained, "Young people are putting their health at risk by smoking and drinking too much."*

- They use indirect or reported speech.

> *Mr. Jones explained that young people are putting their health at risk by smoking and drinking too much.*

A play script with an environmental theme. What does the writer want you to sympathize with?

Scene 1

(It's a hot summer day and lots of people are picnicking, swimming in the river or sailing their boats at Rushford Lakes Country Park. They haven't seen the warning sign that says it is dangerous to swim in the river. Ian and Chris are friends on a bike ride. They stop to look at the river.)

Ian:	Isn't it great to have a day off school?
Chris:	Look at the ducks on the river. Over there are some swans. They have a fluffy cygnet. Isn't he sweet?
Ian:	I am going to feed them with some scraps of bread left over from my lunch.
Chris:	Yes, that's a good idea.

(Chris and Ian throw bread to the cygnet.)

Fisherman:	Hey you! Don't throw bread to the ducks near me. They will swim into my fishing line and snap it off.
Ian:	We can feed the swans wherever we want. Who does he think he is? He doesn't own the river! *(Ian whispers to Chris.)*

(Suddenly a girl races across the road and starts throwing mud at the swans.)

Chris:	Stop doing that. The mother has a young baby and she will attack you.
Girl:	Ha ha ha! I don't care. You're just stopping me from enjoying myself.

(The swan waddles aggressively up towards the girl making a strange noise and raising its wings.)

Girl:	Help! The swan's going to attack me.

(She races across the road to her mom.)

Ian:	That'll show her.
Chris:	The mother swan has just eaten a cigarette butt. I hope it won't hurt her.
Ian:	Have you seen all the rest of the trash people have left behind? Look! There is a plastic bag in the reeds. It could be dangerous to the birds.
Chris:	I counted eight Coke cans and candy wrappers. It's disgusting. Why don't people take their trash home or put it in the cans?

(They get on their bikes and go home for a snack.)

Scene 2

(The sun is setting as Ian and Chris return to give the swans some more bread.)

Ian: It's such a nice evening. I hope the swans are on this side of the river.

Chris: Yes, it will be a pity if they are not. We didn't see them yesterday.

Ian: Look! They're swimming towards us with their cygnet.

(Ian and Chris start throwing bread into the water and the swans greedily gobble it up.)

Chris: Look! He's taking it from my hand. The swans trust us now; they have really gotten to know us.

      Ian, oh no! Just look at his beak: the cygnet is not eating very well. There's something hanging out of his mouth. It's a fishhook. What should we do?

Ian: Can we get it out with a stick?

Chris: No, we might choke him and the mother swan will get anxious.

Ian: We better get the park ranger immediately. He will know what to do.

Chris: We must get help quick, otherwise the baby cygnet might die!

(Ian and Chris run off to tell the park ranger.)

Ian: Chris, do you know which house the ranger lives in?

Chris: No, but we must find him urgently.

Ian:	Look, see that man over there, I think he may be the ranger?

(Ian and Chris walk along the path.)

Ian:	Excuse me, there is a swan down by the bridge with a fishhook in his mouth. Can you give us the number of the swan sanctuary?
Park ranger:	Oh no, not another one! I will call the sanctuary.

(Park ranger makes a call on his cell phone.)

Park ranger:	It has already been reported. They are on their way and will have a rescue team here in ten minutes.
Ian:	We didn't know how we could get it out.
Park ranger:	You did the right thing to get help. Never try to help a bird yourself. It can be dangerous. Where is the swan? Is it the one by the dam?
Chris:	Yes, that's the one over there. You can see it on the horizon.

Scene 3

(Ian and Chris dash back to the bank just beyond the dam.)

Ian:	Can you see the swan family?
Chris:	Yes, they are paddling down the river at a fast pace.
Ian:	We'll try to keep up with them.
Chris:	If we throw bread they'll come. Come on little cygnet, we have some bread for you.
Ian:	Stop over here by these fishermen.
Chris:	My bread is nearly gone.

(Two fishermen and their wives are fishing on the bank. One of the ladies starts feeding breadcrumbs to the family.)

Wife:	Look, what's that hanging out of his mouth? It's a nylon line. How can we pull it out?
Chris:	The park ranger has just called the swan sanctuary and a rescue team is on the way.
Wife:	I have enough bread to keep them here for a while.

(Fisherman's wife feeds the swans. It is getting dark; the sun is setting on the water with a beautiful pink sunset.)

Ian:	I wish they'd hurry up. They are so slow.
Chris:	An hour has passed since we called.
Ian:	Yes, they must be coming by horse and buggy!

(Everyone laughs)

Ian:	It's very dark and late. I think we should go home.

(They say goodbye to the fisherman.)

Fisherman:	I expect they will come in the morning now.

(As they bike up the road, they see a swan sanctuary van.)

Ian:	Look, there's a veterinary ambulance.
Chris:	Yes, it says Ugham Swan Sanctuary

(A lady is sitting on the wall next to the road.)

Ian:	Are you looking for the swan with the fishhook in his mouth?
Lady from Swan Sanctuary:	No, we've got to deal with this fellow first. He's in trouble. He's been sitting on the bank. It's unusual.
Ian:	That's the father swan.

(A few minutes later)

Man in canoe:	We've caught him!
Chris:	I think you've got the wrong one. It was the baby with the fishhook in his mouth. We asked the park ranger to call you!

(The lady on the bank shouts instructions to the man in the canoe.)

Lady from Swan Sanctuary:	Can you see the cygnet? He's coming down on your right.
Man in canoe:	Oh yes, I see him.

Lady from Swan Sanctuary:	He's very scared; he's squeaking.
Man in Canoe:	I think the mother's going to turn on me!
Fisherman:	You saw them too. We waited to see the rescue.
Ian:	Quick, let's go down the river.
Chris:	I can hardly see the swans it is so dark.
Man in Canoe:	*(voice heard in the dark)* I've got the cygnet.
Lady from Swan Sanctuary:	Hold him. I'm coming. Poor little thing, come on, put him in the bag.

(Ian and Chris run up to the group and look at the cygnet.)

Ian:	He's so cute, his little head's sticking out of the bag. Can I stroke him?
Lady from Swan Sanctuary:	Yes, he's not going to like this very much. Come on little one, open your beak. I'm going to try and pull the fishhook out. No, it's stuck and it has cut his throat. Can you see the lump? We will have to take him away for an operation. It costs $100 every time the vet operates!
Wife:	Will he survive?
Lady from Swan Sanctuary:	Yes, he will be fine.
Chris:	Will you bring him back to his mother?
Lady from Swan Sanctuary:	No, we will keep him in the sanctuary with the other cygnets. They will all be put back on the river together.
Ian:	Will his mother pine for him?

| Lady from Swan Sanctuary: | Yes, at first, but we will put the father back to comfort her. After 48 hours she will forget about her baby.

We have had so many birds with fishhooks in their throat this year. The summer months are awful. People leave litter and hooks everywhere and lots of birds have accidents. How would you like it if you had all this trash left in your home?

The cygnet has a barbed hook in his mouth. It's due to lazy fishermen just dumping their lines on the ground. Things like tin cans and plastic bags also bring death to swans. |
| Ian: | I will never throw trash on the ground again. |
| Lady from Swan Sanctuary: | I'm so glad to hear it. |

Scene 4

(Next day - Ian picks up the phone, after it has been ringing for several seconds)

Ian: Hello

Chris: Hi, it's Chris here. I was wondering whether we should go on a bike ride to Rushford Lakes Country Park again.

Ian: I don't know. The cygnet will not be there to feed, so there's no point.

Chris: We could go and play on the adventure playground.

Ian: Ok then. I'll meet you at your house in five minutes.

(Twenty minutes later they arrive at the park. They ride to the river to see the mother and father swan.)

Chris: Look! There's the little cygnet. The swan sanctuary must have removed the fishhook from his beak without operating. It's great to see the cygnet back with his mom and dad.

(The day suddenly seems less gloomy and the two boys are happy that the family is together again.)

How does the play make you feel?

....
....
....

Do you feel sad and angry? Do you want to do something about it?

....
....
....

Writing to persuade in *poetry*.

By Sophie

Little cygnet,
Crouching low
In the reeds,
Why are you choking?

You look pathetic
Perching there,
A nylon thread hanging
From your open beak.
It looks disgusting
And makes you look
More foolish
Than the other birds.

What has happened
To your soft grey feathers
All tattered and torn?
Why do you stare?
You have a sad look.
You plead with me to help you
But what can I do?

What careless one,
Left you so sick,
So scared,
So desperately hungry,
And unable to help yourself?

What do you want me to do?
Shall I tell that fisherman
Who left the nylon line in the river,
What a stupid,
Careless, selfish individual he is?
That his line has been swallowed,
By a creature innocently feeding,
That his litter, so carelessly abandoned,
Without a second thought,
Has caused such suffering.

I'll tell him to stop and think
How it would feel
If he swallowed his own fishhook.

Writing a *persuasive argument* from the writer's *point of view.*

42 Fairhaven Avenue,
Rushford,
Rushford West,
June 16, 2020

The Editor
Young Times

Dear Sir,

   I am very concerned about the way our rivers are being polluted by fishermen who leave dangerous fishhooks in the water. These cause a hazard to the wildlife that live on the riverbank, because they can get them tangled around their necks or stuck in their throats. If these poor creatures are not rescued promptly, they can choke to death.

A few weeks ago I encountered a cygnet, which had swallowed a fishhook and had the nylon line hanging out of his mouth. He could not eat or swallow, which resulted in him being severely distressed. Luckily, I was carrying my cell phone, so I could phone the swan sanctuary. They are volunteers who care for swans on the river day and night. In a few minutes a rescue team arrived, captured him and took him back to the center for immediate surgery. The next day he was released back into the wild.

<u>Fishermen must be persuaded to take all their old equipment home; they must be made aware of the dangers they leave for birds and small animals</u>. There should be new laws passed to make it illegal to leave fishing equipment lying around and heavy fines or prison sentences to deter fishermen from being careless and irresponsible. More notices must be placed by the riverbanks by the city warning, "Fishermen leaving hooks will be prosecuted." All people must be educated on the dangers of leaving litter: sharp tins which can cut or plastic bags that can suffocate.

<u>If people make an effort to take their garbage home, the riverbank will be a much safer place. The wildlife will be healthy and happy. They will be there for us to enjoy.</u>

Yours faithfully,

Christopher Jones

RUSHFORD LAKES COUNTRY PARK

The Rushford Lakes Country Park is an area of land that is in need of rescue. It is no longer a peaceful place where people come to rest and relax away from their busy lives. Wild flowers do not grow abundantly and the area does not provide a habitat for small animals and birds any more. The lake used to be a home to several species of ducks and herons that could be seen from the shore but they have flown away. You may ask why?

Today, the park is a very different place. People drop litter in the hedgerows. They dump old furniture in the lake, without any thought for the environment! The area is beginning to resemble a rubbish tip. Worse still, groups of youths have taken over the land, racing their motorbikes and playing loud music. Vandals have set fire to old cars. Families do not come anymore. No wildlife remains because they have been driven from their homes.

SAVE OUR PARK

Something must be done. It is not too late to save the park. The area could be turned back into the charming place it once was. A petition has been launched for local people to sign so they can persuade the council to turn the area into a nature reserve that everyone can enjoy.

Write an article encouraging people to sign a petition, pointing out what is happening to the land. How could it be improved? Why should they protect the countryside and sign the petition?

You can think out your answer by answering some of the following questions.

1. What has been launched? Why?

   ....

   ....

2. How are people careless when they visit The Rushford Lakes Country Park?

   ....

   ....

3. Why are teenagers a problem?

   ....

   ....

4. Write down some of the advantages of a nature reserve:

   - safety for animals
   - guided walks
   - nesting boxes for bats and birds
   - information boards

   ....

   ....

5. Can you think of some more?

   ....

   ....

6. Why should we protect the countryside?

   ....

   ....

7. Why should we sign the petition?

   ....

   ....

A local builder wants to buy Rushford Lakes Country Park and build houses on it. Write a letter to the city council persuading them that the park should be made into a nature reserve, not a housing development. You must argue to convince the council that your point of view is right.

For letters remember:

1. Structure your argument into paragraphs.

2. Ask, what is the main point I want to make.

   I am writing to protest/complain about…

3. What evidence supports this?

4. Give an explanation as to why you feel like this.

   The reason for this is…

5. Add some of your own comments.

   Those of us who care say…
   I'm sure the city council…

6. Use the correct ending

   If you write 'Dear Sir,' you must use 'Yours faithfully'
   If you write 'Dear Mr. Jones,' you must use 'Yours sincerely'

7. Use linking words and phrases to link paragraphs.

Some people care more than others. People feel angry when they see land spoiled by trash. Their strong feelings come out in their writing, persuading others to believe their views too.

Can you think of some more emotive issues that people feel strongly about?

Here are some ideas you could develop:

- *A highway is proposed and your favorite outdoor swimming pool will close.*

- *A high-rise building will be built in your historic town.*

- *A turbine is going up at your favorite seaside resort.*

- *The farm where you attend your horse riding lessons will be bulldozed to make way for a housing development.*

Writing to persuade in a _formal letter_ using Standard English (not slang).

14 Tree Drive,
Rushford.
(date) November 21st.

Rushford City Council,
High Street,
Rushford.

Dear Sir or Madam,

I am writing to protest about the plan to build a development of houses on Rushford Lakes Country Park. The people of Rushford remember the park when it was a peaceful place, full of trees and wild flowers, where you could walk on a Sunday afternoon. They are saddened by the fact that the city council has not kept the area clean. They have allowed the park to become an overgrown wilderness, where irresponsible people dump trash and unruly kids race motorcycles. As a result of this, the local residents have signed a petition saying that they want the council to create a nature reserve, not a housing development.

You will be aware that the area used to provide a habitat for many rare birds that built nests in the trees. There was also an abundance of small animals like badgers, mice and voles. During the last few years, animals have disappeared because the bushes where they lived have been choked by old cans, plastic bags and take-out boxes. They have been put in great danger by all this litter. The area encourages lots of disruptive teenagers who play loud music that has frightened the animals away. If the council cleared up the area, the animals could return.

It is very important to look after the environment and protect the wildlife, since many animals are in danger of becoming extinct. Some species of birds are now so rare that we need to provide them with nesting boxes in the trees where they can lay eggs. We could establish a visitors' center with information boards about the animals so children learn to appreciate the countryside. This would be a wonderful facility for local schools to bring groups of children.

We hope that you will change your mind and realize that it will be much more beneficial for this town to have a country park with a nature reserve, where people can relax and breathe fresh air, rather than another development of houses.

Yours faithfully,

(Dear Sir, Yours faithfully; Dear Mr. Jones, Yours sincerely)

Writing to _appeal_ to the reader - pull at their heart strings.

hostel
for the homeless

December 20, 2020

Dear Sir,

As Christmas approaches, the homeless will be struggling for survival on our city streets. Many of them, like Charlie, will be forced to sleep in building doorways, coping with freezing cold conditions. It is a chilling prospect. How would it feel to be in his place?

These people are just human beings like you and me, with the same feelings. They laugh and cry just like we do, but… imagine the pain they feel on a winter's night. They are frozen in the biting winter wind; there is no home to return to. They sense the buzz of excitement as Christmas lights illuminate the streets; they have no parties to attend. Delicious delicacies in store windows tempt them; they have no money to buy food. Homeless people are vulnerable at this time of the year, because of hunger, inadequate shelter and poor health. They need to be cared for, but often they have no loved ones. This Christmas they will not laugh, but cry out in pain, victims of hopeless despair. Isn't this an outrage?

More than this, these people have so much to offer society, but they feel useless because no one listens, their viewpoint is unheard and there is no hope of a job. They face boredom, a lifestyle wandering aimlessly in the subways, carrying their bulky backpacks on their shoulders.

While you are preparing for Christmas, spare a thought for the homeless person. Don't just walk past him or her, but stop and take some small change from your pocket. Don't ignore the man who offers to sell you a magazine, but hand him a few coins. Speak some kind words to him or her. Why not send a check to 'Communicate,' a charity that aims to reach out to the homeless. Remember, just a small donation will provide food and shelter for homeless people. It will make a difference!

Whatever you decide to give, it will be much appreciated.

Make a difference to someone's life this Christmas: Act now!

Another emotive issue! What would it be like to be homeless? This leaflet appeals to people to give money.

Can you find some of these persuasive techniques?

- Rhetorical question to make the reader think

- Words are repeated to make them stand out

- A strong opening encourages the reader to read on

- Evidence supports the writer's viewpoint

- Short sentences add to the effect

- Emotive words stir the reader's emotions

- Pronouns 'we' and 'you' speak directly to the reader and identify with him

- A group of three words grabs the attention of the reader

- Alliteration

- A mission statement from the charity 'Communicate'

HOW SAD!

Lying around street corners.
How sad!

Your dog on a dirty blanket.
So sad!

Trouble is always coming your way.
How sad!

You need some attention but nobody notices you.
How sad!

People pass by laughing.
Making fun of the mess you got yourself into...
But you only long to be loved!
How bad!
How sad!

Repeating words like 'sad' emphasises the point the poet is making, that it is awful that some people are homeless.

Short sentences make us feel sympathy. We must help. We must act now.

Can you <u>spare</u> some change Sir?

You hear
Familiar words
Spoken in a small voice
From the path,
"Can you spare some change, Sir?

Look at me.
See what it's like to be hungry.
Not a penny,
Even to buy a burger.

Look at me.
See what its like to have no home,
Only an old blanket
And a cardboard box,

Look at me
See what it's like to be cold
To feel the biting wind
And the driving rain.

Look at me,
To see what it's like to have no job.
To wander
With no purpose.
To know hopelessness and despair…

Can you spare some change Sir?

The title of the poem is:

> Can you spare some change sir?

The theme or message of the poem is: poverty.

> There is a big gap between the rich and poor people. Those who have plenty of money and possessions don't notice homeless people on the street, who know "what it's like to be hungry." This suggests the rich man is often a selfish individual, who thinks only of himself.
>
> In my opinion, it is important to give our spare change to the homeless, because it seems unfair that some people have so much wealth and others know only "hopelessness and despair." It has made me aware of the conditions homeless people face and how they feel.

Emotive words, like 'hopelessness' and 'despair' make us sympathize with the homeless person. We are shocked to hear these words. We feel angry. We want to help.

Write to persuade:

Hi guys,

Communicate invites you to participate in the annual twenty mile walk across the city, to raise money for our favorite charity. We welcome you all to join us. Bring your friends for a great day out... and you will be doing a very important service for the community *(strong opening statement)*.

Our charity, Communicate, founded 14 years ago, helps all people who find themselves in distressing circumstances. It helps those who have come out of prison, those who are homeless or those who are facing disability of any kind. Our centers consist of trained counselors who offer: a shoulder to cry on, hot meals, a bed for the night, as well as genuine friendship. We really do care for our clients and that is true *(a mission statement)*.

By now you may be saying how do I get involved? It is easy. First, download your sponsor form and get as many sponsors to sign up as you can. Then, you just have to turn up at 9pm, at the entrance of the park, on September 14th. You will be given an official rosette to wear to show you are on the walk *(the writer speaks directly to the reader using 'you')*.

After this, you will start zig-zagging you way along the city, walking over bridges and through the park until you reach the end, where your card will be signed to prove you have completed the walk. Exhausted by the thought of it? You don't need to be; a delicious midnight meal will be served halfway, so you don't run out of energy. You will agree, this is a unique opportunity to see the sights of the city; it is a tourist's dream.

Are you ready to sign up? We really need your support. We need to raise $50,000 for the new center. We need to update some of the existing facilities, like the kitchen. We need young, enthusiastic and energetic people to take part in our walk, so please say yes and don't be discouraged by the thought of those aching joints! *(Use inclusive pronouns 'we' and 'our' to gain the support of the reader)*

Hi guys,

Are you up for volunteer work? *(colloquial language)* If the answer is yes, why not come down and help kids at Fairwood House. Come and get your hands dirty, joining in the painting fun, as you help kids who are overcoming serious disabilities. Are you interested? Does this tempt you?

If the answer is yes, *(repetition)*, come down to the center founded by Mary Matthew, the mother of Oscar, who is deaf. She urges you to volunteer and help the kids. She states, "We need buddies to partner with the youngsters, so they can participate in great activities, like baking cupcakes, making models and that sort of thing."

Three years ago, Alfie helped in the project and he said he was really encouraged by the enthusiasm of the kids. I worked with Jasper, who has Down syndrome; he had an interest in astronomy and he wanted to study the night sky, with the new telescope that he got for his birthday. Every week, I helped him observe the constellations – The Great Bear and The Plough *(anecdote)*. He memorized literally the whole universe *(exaggeration)* and really put me to shame, but I learned a lot and I'm still in touch with him.

If you feel you want to get involved, come down to Fairwood House and following an introductory talk, you will be assigned the student you will work alongside. Together you can make your choice from a long list of activities *('You' is talking directly to the reader)*. There is an extra incentive: tons of free cookies, cakes and ice cream from our state-of-the-art ice cream maker. Ice cream like you've never tasted before: smooth, creamy and delicious *(group of three)*.

This writing is informal, so it contains slang and is used to write in a friendly, casual way.

Remember; when you write to persuade and argue, develop your points for and against, using evidence and giving explanation. You may give your personal opinion in the Conclusion.

A writer that feels strongly about an issue will try to persuade the reader to agree with his or her point of view, by using emotive words, like 'hopelessness,' 'pain' and 'despair.' Often a writer will only give one side of the story. He or she may make you realize how miserable it would be to be homeless. Your conscience will be activated when you read this. You will feel you should help.

They may only give one side of the argument! It may be **BIASED**!

- *The writer will give you some strong reasons why a person should be concerned.*

- *They will say what they think can be done about the problem.*

- *They won't give you the other point of view.*

- *They will make you think their point of view is the only one.*

Would you give a few pennies? Are you persuaded?

A highway is proposed and your favorite outdoor swimming pool will close.

The swimming pool is good because...

- Children need to learn to swim

- There are no pools in the area

- It is a place for families to go

- People relax and buy drinks while they watch the swimming

The highway will be bad because...

- It is dangerous and noisy

- It will pollute the air

- There will be nowhere for families to go

- Children won't be able to learn to swim.

What could the city council do?

- Stop their plans immediately.

- Build the road in a different place.

- Build a new, improved, bigger swimming pool to replace the old one.

Write an article with an introduction, points for and against and ending with a conclusion.

The Action Group says it wants to save the pool and stop the highway from being built. They get lots of support and make a petition.

Save our Swimming Pool

IF YOU DON'T WANT THE HIGHWAY TO BE BUILT, SIGN HERE!

Emily Johnson

Tom Brushwood

Sara N. Schroeder

Mr. & Mrs. Marble

Mr. Matthew

....

....

....

....

....

....

....

....

....

....

By Action Committee

Write a letter to persuade the city council not to close the swimming pool

Address of Council Offices

Greeting

Dear Mr./Mrs.…

Introduce the main point

I am writing to ask the council to reconsider closing the swimming pool. This is a valuable facility to the local residents because there is not another swimming pool for five miles. Many people who have young children will not be able to travel to the nearest pool, especially if they do not have transportation.

Develop the writer's point of view further

In fact, it is essential for the local children to have a pool where they can learn to swim, especially since many of them live close to the river that has dangerous currents. Over the last few years, there have been several accidents where children have fallen in and had to be rescued.

Explain why you feel this way

Moreover, our action group feels so strongly about the closure of the pool they have made a petition ....
....
....

Say what you want the council to do

The council can help by ....
....
....

Yours sincerely,

....

Persuasive _Words_

The swimming pool is:

fantastic	family fun	relaxing	healthy
keeps you fit and healthy	amusing	an excellent meeting place	entertaining
keeps kids off the streets	enjoyable	great exercise	a place to unwind

The highway is:

horrible	polluting	noisy	unhealthy
gives people asthma and other health problems	harmful	spoils the beauty of the area	disturbs the peace
ugly	unsightly		

People are:

fed up	furious	shocked	saddened
outraged	infuriated	miserable	livid
irate	they will miss their pool	angry with the council	

13 Christopher Court,
Rushford.

The Complaints Manager,
Rushford City Council,
15 High Street,
Rushford.

Dear Council Member,

I am concerned about an article I read in today's Evening Post, outlining a new road improvement plan which will cut through our famous swim center. It has a terrace to relax on and it provides an outside pool. This is our 'beach' (being some 40 miles from the coast) and many families come, in summer, to soak up the sun here. Surely in this work oriented society, we need to retain this leisure pool.

At the recent planning meeting, a council member who had visited the pool reported that the water temperature is as cold as the Arctic; in her opinion, it is too cold for polar bears to swim in. This is certainly not the view of local office workers who flock daily to the solar heated pool to unwind on their lunch hours. They swim lengths enthusiastically in our cool, refreshing and exhilarating water. Is that not a good recommendation?

The council insists the pool has served its time, that it is unpopular with local people, that it is out of date – that modern children prefer to participate in virtual sports on the computer! This is a ridiculous attitude; the pool plays an important part in teaching local youngsters to swim and these skills are essential in a town with a deep and dangerous river. There have been several accidents. For this reason, the pool offers a structured swimming course for beginners, improvers and advanced swimmers, with good swimmers being able to opt for a class in personal survival. Besides this, safety is paramount, with a group of dedicated lifeguards patrolling the pool to ensure the children's safety.

In my opinion, the new road is not required, whereas the center is a valuable amenity. We urge you to rethink this plan, so we can preserve our pool. We suggest you shelve these road improvement plans and make funds available for recreational and leisure activities in the town, which keep the community happy, unstressed and relaxed.

Yours faithfully,

Fara

Sean Sweetener has a TV show where he chooses a person for a top job in his company. He gives them tests to see who can work best in a team and has the best skills for his company.

Write a letter saying you would like him to choose you for an internship in his company.

Young people of 15-16 years old are often allowed to do a 2-week internship in a job of their choice, but they don't always get paid.

18 Dandelion Crescent,
West Rushford.

Dear Sean Sweetener,

It is certainly kind of you to shortlist me for an internship in your amazingly successful company. Of course, I know all the ten chosen students will be suitable, but in all honesty, I think you will find that I would be the one who could be the most valuable asset to you, by taking a great interest in the company and helping out where I can.

Next year I will be … and have matured a lot during the last year. In fact I have worked hard preparing for my examinations and have completed many hours of studying, so I hope to see good results. You will confidently be able to leave me in charge of a department. I could work manning the phone line and leave your other staff free to do other important business.

Incidentally, I would be so honored if you chose me. It has always been my dream to work in a large computer company. I have always been seriously interested in computers. In fact, I was surfing the web from three years old. It would be such an exciting two weeks. It would mean so much to me. In addition to this, I have followed your program on TV and I admire you as a person. You have an amazing ability to study people's characters and find the right qualities. You must have excellent organizational skills to be able to set up an international company and make so much money. It would be wonderful to have two weeks to share your vision and to see how you expect your staff to work.

I am certain that you will consider the request of all the young people equally alongside mine. Everyone will have good reason why they should be chosen to do work experience with Sean Sweetener. Seeing you on TV has already encouraged me to get a top job, be more confident and take interest in my schoolwork. Now I hope you will give me this opportunity to prove what a good student I could be doing an internship for you. Whatever the outcome, I will always be a great fan of yours.

Yours sincerely,

Chris Hardworker

PART 2

Structuring and *writing* an <u>ARGUMENT</u>

We are familiar with persuasive language in our everyday lives:

- Advertisements convince us.

- Charity appeals persuade us to donate.

- Public service appeals influence the way we think.

When writing to persuade or argue you must remember…

If you are writing to persuade...	If you are writing an argument...
Start with a strong, opening sentence to introduce your main point. It should catch the reader's attention and make him or her read on.	*You may introduce two points of view. Use techniques like rhetorical questions to get the reader on your side.*
Develop your point of view into four or six paragraphs. Move logically from one point to another to develop the argument.	*Continue to develop your point of view. Make reference to any counter-argument if appropriate, but knock it down so you convince the reader that your point of view is right.*
Conclusion... your final paragraph should be the most persuasive to get the agreement of the reader. Use your most emotive language to round out your argument.	*Identify with your reader. Link your ending with key words in the title.*

Remember:

Use **<u>TOPIC SENTENCES</u>** to introduce each paragraph.

The first line of each paragraph, the topic sentence, explains what the paragraph will be about. The remainder of the paragraph will build up this idea. Use one point for each paragraph.

Use a *variety* of sentences.

1. Use <u>simple sentences</u>

   - *Frizos is a small fast food restaurant.*

2. Use <u>compound sentences</u>

   - *The restaurant sells a range of tasty burgers and it has a selection of golden, tasty fries.*

3. Use <u>complex sentences</u>

   - *After Peter played in the match, he went to Frizos fast food place to get some lunch.*

   - *After Emily performed in the school play, she went to Frizos fast food place to get some lunch.*

   - *Peter Redhead, who belongs to the Rushford Gym Club, buys his lunch at Frizos.*

   - *Emily Rogers, who attends Rushford Community High School, buys her lunch at Frizos.*

   - *Since Emily wants to eat healthily, she often chooses a delicious salad from the menu.*

In addition to this:

4. Use <u>statements</u>

   - *Caterpillars nibble juicy lettuce.*

5. Use <u>commands</u>

   - *Wash lettuce leaves well to remove any creepy crawlies.* (Use of the imperative or a bossy verb)

6. Use <u>questions</u> and <u>exclamations</u>

   - *Yuck! What is that creature in my salad?*

   Note: exclamation point expresses shock, surprise

7. Use <u>good verbs, adjectives and adverbs</u>

   - *The juicy (**adjective**) burger was generously (**adverb**) filled (**verb**) with mayonnaise.*
   -
   - *The famous soccer player skilfully dribbled the ball.*

This passage uses literary devices (rhetorical devices) to persuade the reader.

Are you aware that each day our nation's young people gather together at the fast food restaurant, consuming more and more *(repetition)* juicy burgers that contain enough additives to write a chemistry book? *(This is an example of exaggeration.)*

In the popular seaside town on the south coast you can no longer breathe in the fresh salty sea air. It has been obliterated by the stale odor of frying fat from a newly opened fast food outlet and pungent exhaust fumes from cars slowly crawling through the drive-through *(these are examples of personification and contrast)*.

I'm not saying the nation should all turn into caterpillars and munch crispy cabbage leaves *(this is an example of alliteration)*. After all, these only contain vitamins to make you healthy. If you eat healthy food you will only lower your cholesterol so you will live longer *(this is an example of irony)*. You will not become so obese that you don't fit the summer clothes in your closet because you have eaten too many fries.

Does the nation have a choice? *(This is an example of a rhetorical question)* We can change our habits or face the consequences. TV has shown us repeatedly that if you want to stay healthy and live longer, eat low fat foods, plenty of fruit and vegetables and cut down on those burgers *(this is an example of a climax)*.

- The writer includes the audience to get them on his side, saying 'Are you aware…'

- He uses present tense to make it alive.

- He makes a contrast between the fresh air and stale smell of frying fats.

- He uses alliteration, using words with the same initial sound: 'crispy cabbages.'

- He uses irony, saying the opposite of what he really means: 'these only contain vitamins to make you healthy.'

- He uses rhetorical questions when he asks a question that he expects no answer to: 'Does the nation have a choice?'

- He uses personification when he says 'the cars are crawling,' as if they were human (children).

- He builds up to a climax and makes his point at the end.

- He uses pronouns 'you,' 'we' to make you feel the writer is talking directly to you.

- He uses repetition: 'more and more burgers'

- He uses exaggeration when saying the burgers contain enough additives to write a chemistry book – of course they don't.

- He uses emotive words, to stir up response in the reader: 'pungent,' 'obliterated'

- He uses humor to involve the reader or encourage him or her to read on.

What _techniques_ do we use to write persuasively?

1. Start with a good opening paragraph that captures the reader's attention immediately and draws them in. Use present tense.

   - _'Denties is a revolutionary fruit candy that tastes wonderful but amazingly also cleans your teeth. Everyone agrees its results are absolutely incredible.'_

2. Use quotations from people whose lives have been changed.

   - _"After chewing this candy my teeth were transformed. They were white and sparkling. I would definitely recommend this product." (Amy from Rushford)_

3. Use specific details and scientific terms that impress the reader.

   - _'Our candy's revolutionary formula includes xeptyl, trimperidone, hexyldiphedrine' (fictional words)_

   - _'When tested on 1000 children, 99.9% said they loved the flavor and that their teeth felt cleaner and looked whiter.'_

4. Use emotive words and rhetorical language. Use rhetorical questions designed to make the reader think and make him or her think of his or her own response. The writer does not expect an answer.

   - _'Tooth decay is disastrous.'_
   - _'Is there a better toothpaste than Denties?'_

5. Use amazing adjectives and nouns, strong verbs and adverbs.

   - _'revolutionary formula'_
   - _'whitens wonderfully'_

6. Repeat words and phrases to impact the reader. Repetition creates a rhythm and carries the reader along.

   - _'This candy is so, so, so good'_
   - _'Your teeth feel clean, clean, clean'_
   - _Martin Luther King made a famous speech about equal rights for black and white people and repeated the words 'I have a dream…'_

7. Use figurative language devices, such as alliteration, metaphors, similes and onomatopoeia.

   - _'After eating this candy my teeth were as white as snow and sparkled like dew on the morning grass' (simile)._

8. Use language that addresses the reader directly. Use inclusive pronouns, like 'you,' 'we' and 'our' to identify with the reader.

- *'I'm sure you'll agree that'…*

9. Use good vocabulary.

- *'Denties are superb. They are truly a miracle teeth cleaning candy!'*

10. Use humor.

- *'Yuck! There's a wiggly worm on my brush.'*

4. Use casual language/slang and exaggeration to make the reader believe in what is written.

- *'Don't miss out! Get down to the store today. 'Denties' are literally flying (**metaphoric verb**) off the shelves of your local supermarket as we speak.'*

- *Birds fly so we know this means they sell fast. **

5. Use groups of three ideas, separated with commas.

- *'Denties toothpaste is tasty, delicious and sweet. It has an amazing fruit taste, an unbelievable white glow and a freshness you have never seen before.'*

6. Use presentational devices

- *titles, headings and subheadings*
- *underlining and bordering key issues*
- *bulletpoints*
- *charts, graphs and tables of statistics*

7. To end: use conjunctions, words or phrases to join paragraphs.

- *in fact*
- *to my mind*
- *in my opinion*

Write about any of the following. Use the advice above to help you persuade.

Write an article for a young person's magazine to persuade young people to: eat healthily, clean their teeth regularly, walk their dog often.

<u>*Writing Tips*</u> for writing an argument.

- Plan your argument in a mind map or in a list. Have several points on each side.

- If you use first person, 'I' and 'we,' it indicates strong personal belief. (You will identify with your audience.)

- If you use 'we' and 'our,' it indicates a shared vision.

- 'You' (2nd person) is often used in letters and travel brochures to persuade. (You will draw the reader in, so you have his full attention.)

ASK:

1. Who is the **target audience**?

   Children, parents, workers, adults, older people, sports people and teenagers.

   The <u>tone of voice</u> you use will depend on who your audience is.

2. What is my **purpose** in writing?

3. What **tone** shall I use? Will my writing be formal or informal?

Remember:
ALWAYS READ YOUR WORK THROUGH.

Preparing to write a *balanced argument:*

1. Decide on your point of view.

    Make a bold opening statement.

    Structure your work in paragraphs.

---

2. Develop your point of view.

    Consider the evidence you will use to convince your reader.

    Explain why you think like this - P.E.E. (point, evidence, explanation)

---

3. Now consider any counter argument. This is the opposite view of yours.

    Refer to the opposite point of view (the counter argument) and knock it down.

    When you write to persuade you argue from one point of view.

    Alternatively, you can write a balanced argument and give two points of view - for and against.

---

4. Remember when you put forward both sides of an argument your aim is to look at an issue from different viewpoints, before coming to a conclusion or making up your mind.

    Get the reader on your side. Make him or her sympathetic to your point of view.

    Your final paragraph should be the most persuasive, to convince your reader.

If you found that difficult,

Try writing
your argument
this way:

1. Write a dramatic opening. You may include your first point.

2. Develop your key point, using evidence to convince your reader you are right.

   Use persuasive language when writing the point of view you agree with.

3. Introduce a counter argument. It is the opposite viewpoint. It may be the reader's view. Write down what the opposite view says. Often you will do this to strengthen your own point of view and to show the other side has a weaker argument. Build up this argument and then knock it down by making further comments to back up your own point of view.

4. Conclude your argument by referring back to your point of view. Leave the reader in no doubt about your point of view. Your final paragraph should be the most persuasive to get the agreement of the reader. You can use your most emotive language here to complete your argument.

Now for the difficult part...

There are *different approaches* to writing arguments.

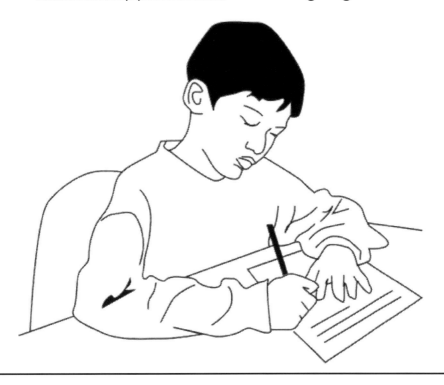

- You can argue from one viewpoint, from a viewpoint you believe in, and develop a series of points.

- Develop your point of view in the first two paragraphs. Refer to the opposite view point briefly in paragraph 3 (this is called a counter argument), but only to strengthen your own case and to show the other side has a weaker argument.

- You can give the counter argument and then argue against it. Make a second point for the counter argument and then argue against it and so on, giving more evidence to support your own view.

- You can begin your argument with an alternative viewpoint and then knock it down, using your point of view.

- You can refer to the counter argument at any point in your own argument.

Brainstorm your ideas:

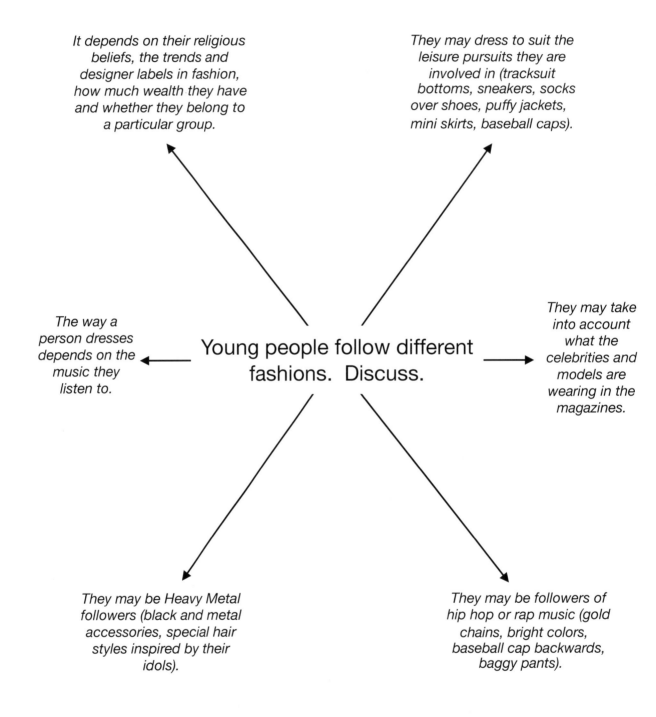

It depends on their religious beliefs, the trends and designer labels in fashion, how much wealth they have and whether they belong to a particular group.

They may dress to suit the leisure pursuits they are involved in (tracksuit bottoms, sneakers, socks over shoes, puffy jackets, mini skirts, baseball caps).

The way a person dresses depends on the music they listen to.

Young people follow different fashions. Discuss.

They may take into account what the celebrities and models are wearing in the magazines.

They may be Heavy Metal followers (black and metal accessories, special hair styles inspired by their idols).

They may be followers of hip hop or rap music (gold chains, bright colors, baseball cap backwards, baggy pants).

What makes young people follow fashion? Discuss

As young people, you have never been so fashion conscious. In past times you would have been content to dress like your parents, but this is certainly not the case in today's image conscious society. As teenagers you have a wide selection of styles to choose from. But what is it that influences you to keep up with all these latest trends?

Let's consider some incentives you may look for when buying clothes. If you are a fashion conscious young person, you may want to adopt the style, however outrageous, of that worn by a famous celebrity on screen, a pop star or even a member of the government. You may want to replicate their look: their haircut, clothing and accessories, because you will be seen to be 'cool' to model yourself on their look – even if, like sheep, countless other people are dressed in a similar style. You need to be seen to be following the latest fashion.

However, this urge to wear the 'right look' can only be due to huge marketing campaigns by the fashion industry. They decide on a theme to launch their current trends, some two years in advance, producing a collection, modeling it on the catwalk and submitting the designs to the manufacturers. When the season arrives, these fashions are promoted in huge advertising campaigns, appearing in the media and in glossy magazines, often targeted at the young. We are made aware of the 'must-haves,' so when they appear in our towns, they attract immense interest. The store sells out within an hour of the item going on the store floor. Incredible!

Finally, fashion is also diverse; it comes in many shapes, forms and colors. Many young people dress to identify with particular groups. Some people are required to wear a scarf to cover their head for their religion. Sporty people may wear a tracksuit or T-shirt with a motif. Others may make individual statements to show they are into heavy rock music or hip-hop. These people might choose to wear black, or brightly colored garments, baseball caps, baggy jeans or metal jewelry, while others might be into retro and go for the vintage look.

In my opinion ....
....
....

"Should I try one of Jake's cigarettes?"

Jake: "Go ahead, try one."

Ben: "I'm not sure I should."

Jake: "Go ahead, one won't hurt."

Ben: "Mom will smell the tobacco on me... and well, it might affect my asthma."

Jake: "You won't know unless you try one."

Ben: "No... I'm not going to. I might get hooked."

Jake: "You're sad."

Now, try writing your own persuasive dialogue.

Why do people try drugs, cigarettes or alcohol?

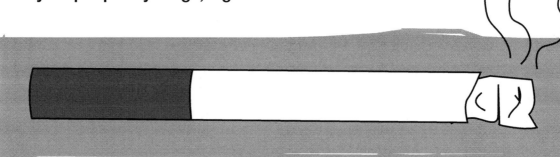

REASONS WHY SOMEONE MIGHT SAY YES:

- Life is stressful.

- Some young people need something to take away the worries of their jobs and their exams.

- It is socially acceptable to smoke with your friends.

- Your friends have started smoking.

- It's cool.

REASONS WHY SOMEONE WOULD SAY NO:

- They are all addictive - especially smoking. You get cravings for them and it is difficult to give up.

- Smoking can cause bad breath, yellow fingers and can cost a lot of money.

- Alcohol makes you do things you wouldn't normally do and this gets you into trouble, like binge drinking. You could also have an accident or make yourself very sick. You could go to the hospital unnecessarily and take up doctors' time.

- Drugs give you big reactions and make you behave differently. TAKING DRUGS IS VERY DANGEROUS. You don't know what they will do to you and can lead to mental illness or worse.

THE LONG-TERM EFFECTS ARE BAD:

- You will destroy your health and put yourself at risk of heart disease, cancer, mental illness and other disease.

- You will look old at a very early age and your skin will become wrinkled up.

- Your teeth will be broken up by all of the acid.

WHAT CAN I DO INSTEAD?

- Take up sports like swimming.

- Go to the gym and exercise.

- Get more interests and join clubs.

- Always say NO to drugs.

- Do not start smoking, because it is difficult to stop.

- Do not drink alcohol until you are an adult and then only drink the recommended amount.

SMOKING MUST BE BANNED.

When you write discursively present both sides of the argument:

1. Introduce the subject.

> *There has been a lot of government legislation about smoking cigarettes. For many years manufacturers have put warnings on their ads, saying that these products can seriously damage your health. Now smoking has been banned in bars and restaurants so people have to go outside to light up. Some people think that smoking should be restricted to a person's home. Should smoking be outlawed in public places?*

2. Write an argument for - include facts and opinions. Work on one side of the argument.

> *For*
>
> *- It looks grown up*
> *- People copy their friends or members of the family*
> *- They think it looks cool*
> *- It's all about their image. They think it makes them look good but does it?*

3. Write an argument against - include the other side's view of the argument. You should present a balanced view of the argument.

> *Against*
>
> *- It leads to adult diseases*
> *- Hair, skin and breath smell of smoke*
> *- It affects breathing and makes you unhealthy*
> *- It makes you stressed*
> *- It wastes a lot of money*

4. Write a conclusion, or alternatively, you may give your own opinion.

> *Conclusion*
>
> *I think smoking is a disgusting habit because it makes people's lungs full of black tar and ...*

Example of a student's work

The government in Europe has decided that it is antisocial to smoke in public, so it is banned in restaurants or public places. People can only smoke on the street or in their own homes. Are young people in danger of damaging their health by smoking?

Smoking can be very harmful. It makes your hair smell of smoke and your fingernails turn yellow. It is a very addictive habit that you can't stop once you start. The worst thing is that if you smoke over a long period of time you will put your health at risk, turning your lungs black which may lead to breathing problems, serious chest infections or lung cancer. Smoking is very expensive and you will waste a lot of money. More than this, smoking affects others. People become passive smokers when they breathe in fumes and risk developing the same diseases as smokers.

Of course, some young people believe that smoking is a good image to have. They think it is cool to hold a cigarette between their fingers as they sit chatting with friends. They are under the impression that it will help them de-stress, unwind and relax and they deny the terrible dangers associated with smoking.

In my opinion, it is safer not to smoke so as to avoid these terrible chest problems, like asthma. It is a disgusting habit, because it makes your teeth yellow when you smile and you may get a bad cough. You will not be able to run fast or participate in sports without getting out of breath. It is better to have the money to spend on other treats like a can of Coke or a box of cookies.

IN FAVOR OF ZOOS OR NOT...

Read the notes. Now write yourself. Discuss the statement in four paragraphs. Remember, you will need an introduction.

For

- Rare animals are protected.

- Breeding programs are carried out.

- Scientists can study the behavior of animals more closely.

- The general public can view animals that they would not normally see.

- They are educational.

- Sick animals are given veterinary treatment.

- They are safe from predators.

- They are given the right food and health supplements – vitamins and minerals, so they grow strong and healthy.

- Most of the animals in zoos are kept in large open spaces.

Against (present the opposite view)

- Putting an animal in a cage is like putting it in prison.

- Animals are homesick for their natural habitats.

- Capturing animals to take them to the zoo is cruel.

- Transporting them by boat, truck or plane is also cruel.

- Animals feel threatened by humans always looking at them.

- If animals are taken from the wild, there will be few left to breed naturally.

- They will forget how to fend for themselves and get lazy. The lions will wait for food rather than hunting for it.

Conclusion

- Weigh up the points, adding your own opinions.

Join the debate. Read the following article that appeared in a magazine.

Since the creation of the first public zoos at the beginning of the nineteenth century, thousands of people have traveled to zoos to marvel at the exotic animals on show within the cages. Yet, it is increasingly being questioned whether zoos are outdated and cruel: should wild animals still be kept in captivation in the 21st century?

There are hundreds of zoological parks in the country with a wide diversity of species in them. They attract an enormous number of visitors every year, being a favorite place for school visits and perfect for family outings.

Giraffe Enclosure

The modern zoo, however, is not just about display; it aims to conserve and educate, playing an important part in protecting endangered species. Some people, though, are angered by the way the animals' movements are restricted by these small enclosures and believe it is cruel to keep them in captivity. Is it right to keep wild animals behind bars?

Zoos present a unique opportunity for the general public to watch the antics of wild animals firsthand. Words cannot describe the incredible experience of seeing the elephants bathe, the mischievous gorillas play, or hearing the lion roar for the first time.

Yet, perhaps more importantly, zoos play an important role in protecting and conserving endangered species, for example, running crucial breeding programs and funding scientific work. Animals are well cared for in our zoological parks, with many zoos committed to realistically recreating the natural habitats of each species, housing them in large open spaces. Their diet is

carefully regulated and the right food is given to them full of all the essential vitamins and minerals they require.

On the other hand, there is the question of whether it is wrong to keep wild animals in captivity. Is it really right to keep them locked up when their natural instinct is to roam free? For some, the answer is definitely no. The Captive Animals Protection Society argues that zoos are effectively part of the entertainment industry and that it is cruel to seize animals from their natural habitats and imprison them in small enclosures for human amusement.

Zoos might claim that their role is to conserve, educate and research but in reality, they are doing more harm than good, with the captive animals showing symptoms of intense boredom and frustration. For example, the imprisoned lions spend their time pacing their cages, unable to enjoy the freedom of the Savannah grasslands. The lion, though, is at least endangered. Some animals held within zoos, such as the giraffe,

are not in danger of extinction so why keep them in such restricted conditions?

It is clearly apparent that this debate raises some seriously emotive and controversial questions, in which both sides make valid points. Are we really any closer, then, to determining whether zoos should be a part of today's society? It might seem selfish, but in a time when most people cannot afford to visit the homelands of these unusual species, I believe zoos play an extremely important role in making people aware of the wonderful world in which we live.

Does it worry me that by holding this opinion I might be depriving these creatures of life in the wild for my own amusement? Of course it does, but as long as we ensure that each zoo is regularly inspected, that all of the animals have large, spacious cages, that resemble their natural homeland, and are treated well, then we will be doing our utmost to guarantee that the creatures in captivity have as good a life as those in the wild.

Write a report arguing whether hosting an international sporting event like 'The Olympics' is beneficial to the country.

Brainstorm the idea.

1. Introduce the subject.

2. Develop the writer's viewpoint.

- There will be more money available from the government and sponsors to encourage young people to take up sports (You could find some statistics to back this up online).

- There will be improved sporting venues with better facilities – for spectators and sports players, which will encourage people to get involved in sports.

- People will generate more team spirit for supporters and competitors. It will foster a competitive spirit.

- People may realize the importance of participating in sports, that it is an essential lifestyle choice to maintain physical fitness – a healthy heart and to avoid obesity.

- The economy will benefit, because supporters that travel to sporting events will spend money in hotels, restaurants and stores in close proximity to the venue, so they will profit. Public transportation will also see a rise in users. During the duration of an international event, there will be countless job opportunities for local people.

- Besides this, sporting venues usually constructed in run down areas will experience a facelift, which will improve life for local residents.

3. Present the opposite viewpoint.

- The euphoria of an international event like 'The Olympics' will be short lived, while people will not take up sports in great numbers because the cost of training and equipment will be too high.

- As well as this, people are too busy managing their stressful daily routines to find the time to start training for sports. Time will be at a premium, leaving no spare minutes for sports.

- Those people who consider exercise important for a healthy lifestyle already attend a gym.

- It is inappropriate for the government to sponsor sports projects when the economy is poor and aid is needed throughout the world – for crises: wars, famines and disasters. Money can be put to better use, to help social welfare.

4. Give your own interpretation (opinion)

I believe ....
....
....
....
....
....

Example of a child's work

REMEMBER THE OLYMPICS 2012; WHAT LEGACY DID IT LEAVE BEHIND?

In the months prior to the 2012 Olympics, there was a great deal of negative belief that Britain would not be able to host such a high profile event. In retrospect, however, there is no doubt that Britain hosted one of the greatest events in history. Every aspect of this prodigious event received positive media coverage and it infiltrated into every corner of the world. The 2008 Chinese Olympics were a hard act to follow, but Britain took the event to a whole new level. This followed on from the sparkling Diamond Jubilee of Queen Elizabeth II; the eyes of the world were fixed on Britain. When the time came, people flocked there in thousands, spent money in their shops, restaurants and bars and used their public transportation system, boosting the economy. Could anyone have asked for a better year?

<u>When the architect's plans for the Olympic Village were revealed, some feared that certain communities would be broken up by the changes.</u>
They feared people would be re-housed, they would be separated, they would see their businesses destroyed. On the contrary, what actually occurred can only be termed positive; the inventing and remodeling of a rundown industrial site created the spectacular technological innovation that is the Olympic Park. It was an area of wasteland and it was totally transformed. Stadiums appeared at the wave of a magic wand: an aquatic center, shops, restaurants and accommodation for athletes. Surely these facilities will benefit future generations of sportsmen and women.

<u>Before the event, some people argued that London would never be</u> <u>able to cope with an event on such a large scale, with such an influx of</u> <u>visitors.</u> They stated it would be a strain on public services; that the transportation system wouldn't cope and there would surely be a risk that crime rates would increase. In reality, the city, a place of cultural diversity, came together for a week long celebration and the streets, avenues and alleys were decked with colorful flags, as if a canon had fired balls of red, white and blue across them. Together, thousands of city dwellers watched incredible sporting events on communal screens. Huge cheers expressed their joy, as their heroes passed the finishing line to gain gold. These images, of their champions receiving these glorious gold medals on the podium, still remain fresh in their minds. As the nations cheered on their teams, supporting their countries, we saw a community spirit rekindled.

<u>What is more, these memories prove those wrong who insisted the</u> <u>Olympic legacy would be short lived and that people would soon forget.</u> This event certainly impacted the whole country. It promoted a message that competitive sport is still good and that it is possible to train to play a sport whatever your age, gender or ability. As a result of this, sponsors have been providing training programs and equipment to encourage young people to get involved in sports and at the same time benefit from a healthier lifestyle: to get fit, to take care of their hearts and to avoid obesity. Sports are a good lifestyle choice.

In conclusion, the 2012 Olympics appeased <u>those cynics who stated it</u> <u>would not be beneficial to fund an international event of this dimension</u>. They pointed the finger to where the money could be better spent: providing aid to countries torn apart by war, poverty, famine, and natural disasters (and not to forget issues closer to home, like health care). To my way of thinking, the Olympics were money well spent. It was hugely beneficial and it touched the hearts of the people. It changed the way many think about sports. I was impressed by the commitment of the athletes, bowled over by the teamwork demonstrated and the way the whole event was coordinated, from the flamboyant opening, to the closing ceremony. Even the media coverage, bringing events live to our homes, was outstanding. Our wholehearted support brought many people closer together around the world.

ELDERLY PEOPLE IN OUR SOCIETY ARE NOT TREATED WITH VERY MUCH RESPECT. DISCUSS

<u>Elderly people are not always given the best care in our society because:</u>

- People can neglect older relatives.
- In the hospital, their treatment is delayed because they're too old.
- Their views are not listened to.
- Unscrupulous contractors trick them by overcharging them.

<u>We can help by:</u>

- Inviting them over or visiting them.
- Taking them meals or doing the shopping.
- Making sure they're comfortable.
- Making sure their homes are well heated, as old people can get seriously ill in the winter from being cold (hypothermia).

<u>What experiences have you had of older people?</u>

- Collecting and delivering gifts at elementary school during festivals.
- Putting on concerts for elderly relatives and neighbors.

<u>How should the community treat old people?</u>

- Treat them with respect.
- Listen to them.
- Take advice from them because they have many years of experience.

<u>What needs to happen to improve the lives of older people?</u>

- Provide old people's homes with better facilities.
- Employ more people to help old people in the community.
- Bring old and young people together socially for activities in schools and clubs. Some awards actually encourage young people to work with the elderly – talking to them and playing games as part of the community service award.

Example of a child's work

In the future, our country will have more and more elderly people who have reached the age of 80+. There are growing numbers of people who live to be one hundred years old. All these people have worked hard for their country. Some of them have served in the armed forces and some of them have been in caring professions like nursing. In today's society, do we really give them the support they need when they get older themselves?

In the 21st century elderly people benefit because they are living longer. They have a good diet and have the benefits of modern drugs that can treat the illnesses that they develop as they get older. It is a sad fact, however, that in newspapers, we read terrible stories about old people who have been left on stretchers in hospital halls because there are no beds in the wards. Mr. … went into the hospital with dizziness at the age of 94, but there was no bed for him, so he spent three days in a hallway. When his son complained, the hospital forced him to travel a hundred miles in an ambulance to a hospital in another area (anecdote – using a a short, personal example). It seems that this man did not get the treatment he needed because he was considered too old.

In the newspapers we read about old people who are desperately lonely because they live far away from their children or their relatives who do not have time to care for them. However, there are many people who devote much of their time to caring for elderly people, helping them with their daily chores like mowing the lawn or shopping. There are also some schools that collect cans of food to deliver to elderly people, while other young people visit local nursery homes and perform concerts. Despite this, there are still many isolated and elderly people who watch T.V. all day, who never have a visitor, never go to a social event. It is these people who we have a responsibility to reach. We could go over to visit and talk or even take them a meal. In the cold weather we can make sure they are warm, safe and comfortable in their homes and not in danger of getting serious illnesses, like hypothermia.

From another point of view, there are unscrupulous workers who prey on elderly people demanding large sums of money for jobs badly done. This all seems scandalous. However, some would say that these stories are media hype and that unfortunate people have these experiences at any age whether old or young. Generally old people are well cared for.

In my opinion, old people in our society have a lot to offer. We should listen to their views because they have a great deal of experience about life issues. We should build amazing old people's homes with modern facilities at a cost that everyone can afford. We should learn to respect our senior citizens and get rid of the stereotypical image that people live past their expiration date and have nothing left to offer.

Emotive words

Emotive adjectives persuade and make people feel interested in or feel sympathy for…

astonishing	amazing	huge	massive	detestable
catastrophic	awful	disastrous	terrible	shocking
diabolical	preposterous	horrendous	vile	hateful
remarkable	incredible	astounding	wonderful	miraculous
surprising	startling	mind-blowing	unbelievable	inconceivable
staggering	appalling	dreadful	unbearable	horrifying
atrocious	unspeakable	horrific	hideous	repulsive
nasty	disgusting	intolerable	fantastic	bizarre
extraordinary	terrific	superb	marvelous	brilliant

Can you think of any more?

Linking words and phrases

despite	however	moreover	nonetheless	on the other hand
but	on the contrary	in fact	according to	in my opinion
most people agree	even though	in some circumstances	nevertheless	you could say
I'm sure you'll agree that	in addition	furthermore	what is more	besides
also	additionally	likewise	personally	for my part
yet	still	then again	in spite of this	in contrast
alternatively	except	excluding	including	save for
although	while	even if	even supposing	in fact
in some cases	certainly	in reality	in effect	really
in truth	indeed	definitely	without doubt	

PART 3

Time to _practice_

Use the next pages to practice writing persuasively and to write arguments.

Write a brief review on a film, T.V. program or book you have seen/
read recently. Persuade the audience why they should see the film or
read the book. You can choose your favorite soap, T.V. episode or film.

Use the following questions to help you:

- _What is the story line?_
- _What is the plot?_
- _Where is the setting?_
- _Who are the characters?_
- _Are the characters believable?_
- _Can you identify with them?_
- _Does it have a strong opening?_
- _Does it have a satisfactory ending?_

- _What is its purpose?_
- _Does it entertain?_
- _Is there humor?_
- _Is it full of action?_
- _Does it build up dramatic suspense?_
- _Does it keep the reader on the edge of his or her seat?_
- _What genre does it take? Is it a cartoon, a horror film or a thriller?_
- _What audience does it appeal to? (teenagers, adults or children)_
- _Does the film have good visual effects?_
- _Is it colorful with good animations?_
- _Is it fast moving?_

- _What is your personal view of the film?_

The school board will pay for one person to go on the vacation of their dreams. Only one person will be chosen. Where would you like to go?

Write the reasons why you would like to go:

- hot and sunny

- fun

- relaxing

- once in a lifetime experience

- ....

- ....

- ....

- ....

- ....

- ....

- ....

Write a letter to the school board persuading them to choose you.

Dear Mr. …….………,

How kind of you to pay for a young person from this school to go to…..
……………………………………………………………………………………
……………………………………………………………………………………

Although we would all like to go, I feel I would be the most suitable
person to choose because …………………………………………………
……………………………………………………………………………………
……………………………………………………………………………………

Now that I am ………………………….. I am capable of…………………….
………………………………………… so you wouldn't need to worry about me.

I would be ………………………………………………………………………
…………………………… (independent, reliable, able to look after myself).

I am looking forward to going on this trip because I want to see ………..
……………………………………………………………………………………

I have always wanted to visit …………………………………………………
……………………………………………………………………………………

It would be wonderful to ………………………………………………………
……………………………………………………………………………………

Finally, this trip promises to be a vacation of a lifetime. When I get
back I will have learned …………………………………………………………

End
I would like to have the opportunity of saying thank you for ……………..
……………………………………………………………………………………

Yours sincerely,

…………………….

You invited your friend to your birthday party but she has refused the invitation. Write back trying to persuade her to change her mind.

The Old Farmhouse,
Sheep Way,
Rushford.

Dear Amy,

Main point

I am seriously disappointed that you have not accepted the invitation to come to my birthday party on Saturday. I know you would have really enjoyed it. You would also have had the opportunity to meet my cousin from New Zealand who is staying with us for a few weeks. A number of school friends will also be coming to celebrate.

Develop Idea

Is there any chance that I can persuade you to change your mind? I realize that your exams are approaching and you have a lot of studying to do. However, our teachers have advised us that we should only study for a few hours at a time, then take a break. It is good to have a change of scenery so that when you return to your work you will be refreshed.

Comment

Of course I am concerned about you as a best friend. If you stay indoors too long sitting in a chair, you will become like a couch potato and may put on weight or get unhealthy by having too little exercise. Added to this, there are few interesting programs on TV during the summer months, especially on a Saturday. I am only giving you this advice to make you realize what a special event you are missing. I hope I will not offend you, as you are a very good friend.

Now I would like to give you this opportunity to change your mind. Come to the party and help us eat all the delicious food my mom is preparing and dance, dance, dance till late in the night. You will definitely have a super time. Look forward to hearing from you.

Yours affectionately,

Lucy

Can you find which persuasive devices are in the text?

Discuss the following statements in four paragraphs:

1. Introduce the subject
2. Develop the viewpoint
3. Refer to the opposite viewpoint
4. Sum up, giving your own interpretation or opinion.

ANIMALS SHOULD PERFORM IN THE CIRCUS...

Introduction

At a well-known international circus that travels around the world, a dozen lions come into the circus ring. They sit on stools and perform tricks, rising on to their back legs. The trainer takes food from a lion's mouth. Horses rise up on their hind legs and let riders do acrobatics on their backs. The audience is warned not to stretch their hands out when a trainer brings in the tiger on a rope. He walks slowly around the edge of the ring. The audience gasp in awe. It is awesome to see how the trainers have tamed these wild cats; have made aggressive creatures obey them like domestic kittens; have taught routines to creatures that have the ability to pounce on humans and rip them to pieces. Some people think it should be illegal to use wild cats in circuses, because it is considered to be cruel to keep such large animals in cramped conditions for human pleasure. Are we missing out on some thrilling entertainment? Should animals like lions or tigers be allowed to perform in the circus?

Points For

- In many countries it is traditional for traveling circuses to have a zoo, which they also open to the general public.

- It is thrilling to see wild cats working with people.

- In all circus acts there is some risk. An acrobat can fall, a lion could pounce, but people go to the circus to be thrilled and to see risky acts that no one else can do.

- Animals enjoy their work and like performing in front of an audience. They have a good relationship with their trainers or else they would not obey them or learn the tricks. Dominique, the owner of the Marlette Circus, shakes paws with the lions through the cages.

- Other animals work, cows are milked, horses are used by the police or army and elephants carry logs.

Points Against

- It is extremely cruel to coop up big animals in a small cage that is close to other animals and which restricts their movements.

- They are forced to travel long distances in cages that are often smelly and unclean.

- They do not get enough exercise and they miss the huge savannahs in Africa - their natural habitat. They might be homesick.

- They forget how to fend for themselves.

- It is cruel to force animals to learn tricks. Some trainers are harsh and cruel, using whips to make their animals obey them.

- Animals cannot say 'no' and express their feelings, so the trainers are taking advantage of them.

Write a conclusion - adding your own opinion

1.	2.
In my opinion it is very entertaining to experience the atmosphere of the circus with performing animals. When the lions and tigers march in to music they seem to be very content and love to show off to the audience. They wag their tails in appreciation when they hear the audience cheering. The relationship between the trainers and animals seems to be good. They seem to love their animals. I am in support of allowing animals to perform in circuses.	It is absurd to bring 'killer' creatures into a circus when young children are watching. Only last year, a boy fell into a pit at a zoo and was badly mauled by a fierce lion. These animals can suddenly become ferocious and turn on humans. They may attack members of the audience. As far as I am concerned, it is not worth the risk for the sake of entertainment. Wild cats should be kept behind bars or left to roam in their natural habitats.

Remember, use joining words:

however   *moreover*   *on the other hand*

Read the notes. Now you can write. Discuss the question.

SHOULD FOX HUNTING HAVE BEEN BANNED?

In some parts of the world, like England, fox hunting was a tradition. Many riders went out to hunt foxes on holidays or other special occasions. A pack of hounds or dogs ran alongside the horses to chase and kill a fox – it was a sport. The British government has banned fox hunting because it's a blood sport. This decision has left people divided and some people still believe it was a bad choice. What do you think? Should fox hunting have been banned? Discuss in four paragraphs.

Write an Introduction

The hunt was a tradition that went back through many centuries. Many experienced riders would take part. They would wear the traditional red coats that their ancestors had worn for generations and blow hunting horns. A pack of hounds, consisting of small dogs called foxhounds, would run alongside the horses, chasing a fox until it was caught and killed. This was known as a blood sport because the victory of winning ended in the horrific, cruel death of an innocent creature. It is a fact, for the sake of a few hours of enjoyment, a poor creature suffered. However, some people feel it was unjust for the government to ban the sport, which many people enjoyed participating in. Should fox hunting have been banned?

Points For

- It is a chance for riders to meet socially.

- To practice their riding skills in a team working together.

- To participate in a 'sport' that people had been doing for hundreds of years.

- Wear cool red hunting jackets.

- Part of countryside tradition.

- Thrilling experience for the riders, horses and even the fox, which enjoyed the run and sometimes got away.

Points Against

- It is an outdated sport, barbaric, cruel and vicious.

- A pack of hounds chase one poor fox.

- It encourages the dogs to kill. They catch the fox, drag it under the hedge and rip it apart with their sharp teeth.

- People who go on these hunts are allowing suffering. They are permitting the murder of poor innocent animals.

- The fox cannot say no and he cannot speak for himself. He feels only terror, at the noise, the chase and fear of losing his life.

- Cubs may be orphaned.

Conclusion

In my opinion, the hunt is a very colorful tradition but it should remain a thing of the past. The riders in their traditional costumes are taking part in a tradition that has been practiced for generations. However, the suffering the fox goes through is barbaric. We do not treat people in this way, so why should we allow poor innocent animals to be abused like this? Maybe an artificial fox could be used; otherwise, it would be better to concentrate on other horse riding events such as show jumping...

Read the notes. Now you can write. Discuss the question.

CHEWING GUM MUST BE BANNED FROM PUBLIC PLACES LIKE SHOPPING MALLS AND SWIMMING POOLS

Introduction   **Add your own ideas.**

There are many people who find it comforting to chew gum. It may be that 'chewing' helps them feel less stressed as they go about their lives. Others feel it is better to chew gum than smoke or eat unhealthy chocolate bars and candy that is full of sugar and will rot their teeth. There are many people who would say it is an antisocial habit because it is unpleasant to talk to someone who is chewing gum. It is even more disgusting to put your hand on someone else's gum under the desk. Is there anything worse than finding a piece of gum on the bottom of your shoe? Should chewing gum be banned from public places?

For Banning Gum

- People leave gum on chairs, in changing rooms or on the streets and it turns solid, leaving black marks on the path which you cannot remove without a special cleaner. This makes the streets look messy and dirty.

- Someone has to be employed to clean up gum stained paths, which is a waste of city money that could be spent on something else.

- It is unpleasant to talk to people chewing gum.

- It is unhealthy for the teeth and the gums. Explain why...

- It is a bad habit, like a young child wanting his pacifier.

For Not Banning Gum

- People buy sugar free gum that cleans your teeth and freshens your mouth.

- It helps people concentrate.

- People should be able to choose whether they chew or not as long as they put the finished gum in the garbage.

Conclusion...

I think it should be up to ....   I agree that ...   I disagree ...

92

Read the notes. Now you can write. Discuss the question.

CHILDREN UNDER FOURTEEN ARE TOO YOUNG TO TAKE EXAMS

Introduction   **Add your own ideas.**

Some teachers and parents believe children under fourteen should not be put under the pressure of taking exams. Some schools have opted out of exams, because they argue that children need the time to grow up and play outside in the fresh air, rather than staying inside and cramming for exams. When they reach high school, they will have to work hard preparing for exams in their classes as well as SATs. Other people think it is very important to start working hard from a young age in order to get good results that will lead to a good job. Is it necessary for children under fourteen to start thinking of their future?

For

- It is important to learn Math, English and Science so you get a good job.

- Tests help you know how much progress you are making.

- The results of tests help you to see if you are doing as well as your classmates.

- They help your teachers to put you in the right group.

- If you learn good working habits when you are young, it will help you do well on your SATs.

- Doing extra work helps you learn more so you will be ahead of your classmates.

Against

- Children work hard in school and they have a lot of homework so they can't go out to play in the fresh air.

- They miss out on playing games and sports, joining clubs, making friends and going on outings because they have to work.

- Schools are sometimes too busy doing work to organize school trips.

- Being clever is not just about tests; some children are better at art, music and drama.

Conclusion...

I think exams help you to see how well you are doing in school and where you are in the class, but I think teachers shouldn't spend so much time giving tests because ...

Read the notes. Now you can write. Discuss the question.

SCHOOL UNIFORMS ARE A GOOD THING?

Introduction   **Add your own ideas.**

When the school day has finished, it may be easy to recognize which school students have come from by the uniforms they're wearing. Some schools have uniforms, which can be in different colors, styles, and logos. Most children look well put together and neat in their uniforms. However, in some schools, children are not required to wear uniforms or dress identically; instead they can choose their own casual outfit to go in. In stores, there is a big choice of clothing to choose from, some by designers. Is it better if everyone wears the same clothing? Would it become too competitive if you had to dress up for school everyday?

For

- They make you look neat, sharp, and give you an identity.

- You don't have to choose something to wear each morning, so you're not late for school.

- Everyone wears the same clothes so you don't have to compete with other children to see who has the latest fashions or designer labels.

- You don't have to do so much shopping and it will save your parents money.

- School uniforms are made of tough, washable fabric so you don't spoil your own clothes.

Against

- Everyone looks the same and there is no scope for individuality.

- Uniforms are expensive.

- It is old fashioned and outdated to wear a uniform - a thing of the past.

- Uniform is not as comfortable as your own clothes.

Conclusion...

I like wearing a school uniform because I know what I'm going to put on each morning. I don't have to worry. However, school uniforms would be better if they were more fashionable and up-to-date. For example, the schools could have their own school uniform designers, to design suitable stylish clothes.

DO YOUNG PEOPLE EAT TOO MUCH FAST FOOD?

Write a balanced argument.

Remember:

- Introduce your subject

- Develop your point of view

- Refer to the opposite point of view or counter argument briefly, but knock it down using your own point of view.

- Take another point from the counter argument and knock that down with your point of view and so on.

- Use stylistic techniques.

- Sum up, making your last paragraph the most persuasive to convince the reader your point of view is right.

Notes on: Why do people need to choose fast food?

Use these notes to write your own argument.

For

- People are under pressure to do everything quickly so there <u>is no time to cook meals and it is easier to get a burger</u>.

- There is <u>no dish-washing</u> or mess to clean up. Burgers and fries come in disposable packaging.

- You can talk to your friends while you eat. Fast food restaurants are <u>a warm, safe environment off the street to meet up</u>.

- Many <u>fast food restaurants now sell salads, fruit, vegetables</u>, yogurts, mineral water and fruit juices as well as burgers and fries.

- <u>Children adore fast food</u>, such as hamburgers and fries.

- Fast food is sold at <u>reasonable prices</u>.

- If you are in the shopping district and you see a familiar fast food sign, you know it will be <u>a reliable, safe place to eat and won't cost too muc</u>h.

- You <u>can go into a fast food restaurant alone and not feel lonely</u> because there will be other people there.

- Fast food restaurants are perfect for families eating with children because they have <u>a relaxed and informal atmosphere</u>. The children can move around and talk loudly.

- It doesn't matter if kids spill food.

- Children usually like fast food.

- Many fast food restaurants do birthday parties for young children.

On the other hand...

Against

- Fast food stops you from trying out cafés and restaurants serving healthier food.

- There is little variety on the menu and people always eat the same thing.

- There are too many people crowded into a small environment, especially at peak times of day. This makes for a very noisy environment.

- It is not good for the digestion to eat too fast and it is important to sit and relax while you eat.

What do the experts say?

- If you eat too much junk food you will not have a healthy diet.

- You will lack essential vitamins and minerals and take in too much fat.

- If you put on too much weight, you might age prematurely.

- For example, your teeth will be decayed by food containing too much sugar.

- If you put on too much weight, you will also get out of breath when you exercise and you will risk severe illnesses like heart disease and cancer.

Write out your argument in four paragraphs.

SHOULD YOUNG PEOPLE EAT MORE FRUITS AND VEGETABLES? DISCUSS

Young people: Do you consider fruits and vegetables to be an important part of your diet?

AGAINST

- They are <u>dull and flavorless</u> compared to highly seasoned fast foods with added fats and sugars.

- They <u>take too long to prepare</u> because you have to wash and peel fruits and vegetables so you cannot eat them 'on the go.'

- They <u>are too messy to prepare and eat</u>. Take peaches, for example - they are very juicy and difficult to eat.

- Fruits and vegetables <u>don't fill you up</u>. After eating them you still feel hungry so your body craves carbohydrates, like bread and cakes that give you energy throughout the day.

- It's <u>not fashionable</u> (among young people) to snack on fruit.

- There <u>are many delicious foods that are far more appealing</u> than fruits and vegetables, like cakes, chocolate, chips and pizza, which are not so <u>expensive</u> to buy.

- You <u>can take multi vitamins in place</u> of fruits and vegetables and get the same nutritional benefit.

- The risk of health problems like cancer and heart disease are a long way off in the future. There may be advances in medicine by then, so you should not worry about the effects of an unhealthy diet.

- Are fruits and vegetables healthy anyway? They <u>are sprayed with fertilizers, pesticides and chemicals. Many are genetically modified.</u> Can we trust them? We are probably better off keeping away from them!

Does eating fruit and vegetables have to be boring?

FOR

- There is more choice of fruits and vegetables than ever before to suit all tastes, occasions and styles of cooking. You can try out really exotic fruits and vegetables – mangos, papayas and passionfruits.

- You can vary your diet according to the season: berries in the summer and clementines in the winter. With so much choice and variety, how could you possibly get bored!

- You can make tasty desserts healthy, by adding ice cream or chocolate sauce to fruit or yogurt. For instance, you can make banana splits, strawberries with cream or dust a little powdered sugar on bitter fruit like grapefruit. Alternatively, you can make fruit smoothies by liquidizing fruit of your choice. You can chop up raw vegetables, such as celery, carrots and cucumber and dip them into salsa and guacamole.

- Fruit is the ultimate fast food because you can eat it raw. It only takes seconds to unpeel a banana

WHAT DO THE MEDICAL EXPERTS ADVISE?

- Fruits and vegetables are full of vitamins, minerals and fiber, which young people need to maintain good health. More importantly they are low in fat. (We don't want people becoming obese.)

- You should follow the 5 a day rule to stay healthy.
- For example, for breakfast you could have a glass of fruit juice and a handful of dried fruits. Try raisins with your cereal. Eat midmorning snacks of grapes or an apple. Have a salad for lunch and vegetables and canned fruit with your dinner. It does not take too much effort to change your diet and eat healthily.

- Fruits and vegetables help to keep your body fitter, healthier and happier. For example, they build up your immune system that helps your body fight off colds, infections and viruses. They keep your complexion healthy, your hair shiny and your nails strong.

Write a letter to your local Congressperson, against the construction of a group of windmills in your favorite seaside place. Discuss in four paragraphs.

1. Introduce the subject.

2. Develop the writer's point of view

- Windmills are large steel structures that use wind to generate electricity.

- They are renewable forms of energy.

- They will never run out of power, whereas non-renewable energy like coal, gas and oil will run out one day.

- We need wind energy to power all our electrical machinery.

3. Present the opposite point of view

- However, big steel windmills are ugly and they spoil the countryside and the seaside.

- People go to the seaside to relax and don't want to have to stare at these steel structures.

- They are dangerous for birds and wildlife because they get caught in their blades.

4. To conclude, offer a solution. Give your own interpretation (opinion).

- Build windmills in places where no one goes.

- Find different ways to make energy.

Now try these:

Write a letter to the city council arguing the fact that the farm where you take horse riding lessons is going to be bulldozed to make way for a housing development. Discuss in four paragraphs.

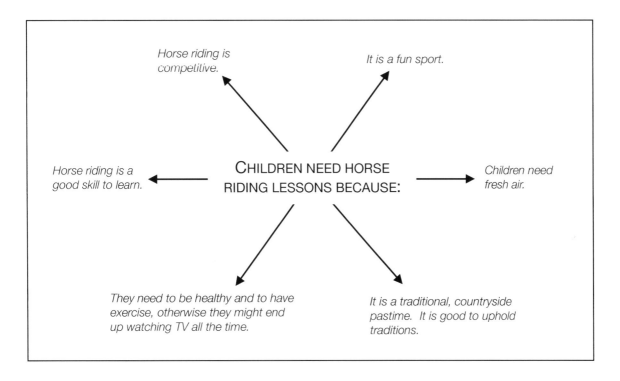

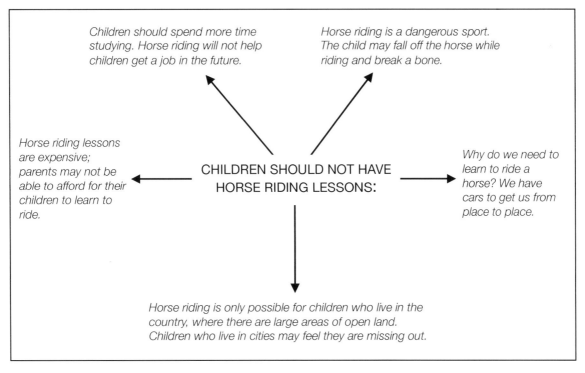

Write a letter to the city council arguing against the construction of a high-rise apartment building that will be built in the historic town where you live. Discuss.

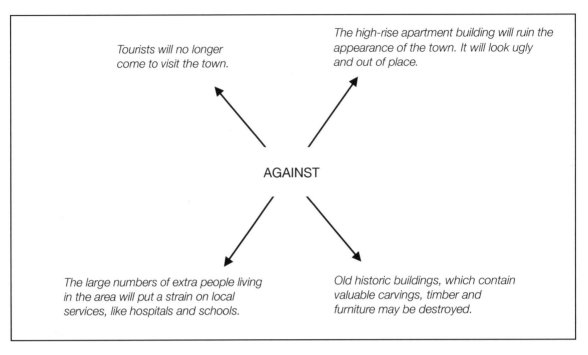

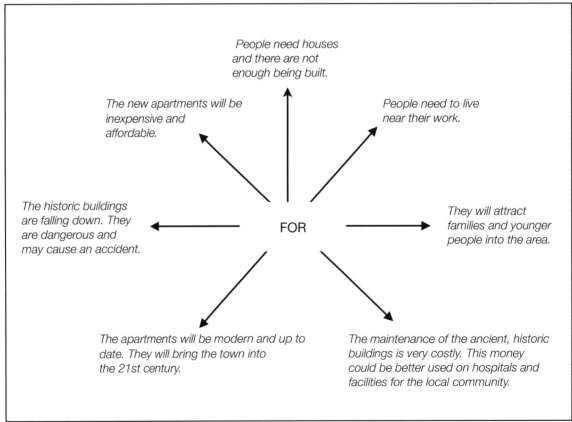

SHOULD PEOPLE BE ALLOWED TO KEEP WILD ANIMALS IN CITY YARDS?

Introduce the subject:

For

- Helping endangered animals
- Assisting conservation work
- Breeding the animals
- Studying them to learn more about them

Against

- Cruel to shut them in small cages
- Dangerous to people and pets
- Noisy and smelly
- Might escape into the neighborhood
- Cages aren't pretty to look at

Opinion

- There's no need to keep wild cats in a yard surrounded by people. You can study them in a zoo or on a safari where they will not endanger the lives of people.

About _Persuasive_ Writing...

Write to:

MAKE HIM OR HER BELIEVE	MAKE HIM OR HER VISIT	CONVINCE THEM
GET THEM ON YOUR SIDE	WIN THEM OVER	MAKE HIM OR HER SIGN
SHOCK THEM	MAKE THEM DO SOMETHING	MAKE THEM BUY
MAKE THEM BOOK A VACATION	MAKE HIM OR HER SAY YES	SUPPORT YOUR CAUSE

Ask:

- What is the writing about?
- How does my reader feel about it?
- What is my message?
- Have I influenced his or her thinking?

Remember: to aim at the higher levels (and grades) you need figurative language.

This includes:

- Metaphors: *'The baby is a little monster.'*

- Similes: *'Emma's kitten was as light as a feather.'*

- Personification – gives things human qualities. They paint pictures and build up atmosphere:

  'The leaves whispered in the trees.'

  'The first light crept stealthily into the room.'

- Analogy: *'Bird is to nest as dog is to kennel.'*

- Alliteration: *'Rachel ran rapidly around the room roaring like a lion.'*

- Onomatopoeia: *'Bang!' 'Crash!'*

- Use **conjunctions** to connect paragraphs, as in *'in fact,' 'to my mind,' 'in my opinion,' 'on the other hand,' 'as a result of'* and *'moreover.'* Remember, when you write persuasively, you aim to convince or influence your reader so they can see your point of view. You aim to change their opinions so they can see you are right.

1. Can you tell the difference between fact and opinion?

   - *'Cats have whiskers' is a <u>fact</u> because it is true.*

   - *'Cats make good pets' is an <u>opinion</u> because it may not be true or only true in the eyes of the writer.*

2. Opinions make people believe a viewpoint.

3. Persuasive writing often presents only one viewpoint.

   - *What is the main idea or message?*
   - *How is the message put across?*

Techniques to help you.

---

1. Use <u>rhetorical questions:</u> to involve your audience and get them thinking, to raise questions in the reader's mind and make him or her think about his or her own response. The writer does not expect an answer but uses them to persuade.

    Isn't it about time we started to consider the future?

    Isn't it about time we started to think about our diet?

    Television might be a part of everyday life, but does it influence us?

---

2. Use <u>humor</u>

    Yuck! There's a caterpillar in it.

---

3. Use <u>repetition</u>, which creates a rhythm and carries the reader along.

    "Puff, Puff, Puff, as much as you can"

    'You can…You can….You can help by sending a check to…!"

    Martin Luther King made a famous speech about equal rights for black and white people and repeated the words, 'I have a dream... I have a dream...'

---

4. Use <u>emotive words</u> to stir up response in your reader.

    After the deluge of rain fell, the horrified inhabitants returned to their flooded houses, to face a scene of disaster and devastation.

    A tremendous cheer sounded as the ball bounced into the goal and the spectators broke into a tumultuous applause.

To GET GOOD GRADES use techniques:

- **Groups of three**

   The path ahead looked dark, dingy and dangerous.

- Use **contrasts** - writing about two opposite subjects.

'The fresh air of the seaside was obliterated by the aroma of fries from the fast food restaurant.'

- Use **anecdotes** or a short, personal story to illustrate a point.

   "Even my Grandma keeps in touch with her friends on..."

- Use **irony,** saying the opposite of what you mean. For example,

   'What a nice day' when it is raining.

- Use **persuasive language** to get the reader on your side:

     - *'we would'*
     - *'we should'*
     - *'we have no doubt that...'*

- Use advanced **punctuation** for effect -   :   ;   ( )

- **Pronouns** like 'we' to get the reader on your side, speaking directly to the reader. Use of the second person 'you' involves the reader.

- **Exaggeration** - Overstating something.

- **Lists and statistics** to emphasize a point.

- **Colloquial language** - informal or slang speech.

- **Quotations** - words spoken by people with knowledge of the subject.

- **Higher level vocabulary** - powerful adjectives, verbs and adverbs.

More topics to explore:

- Does advertising convince us to buy things we don't want?

- Do disabled people have the same rights as able-bodied people?

- Too much loud music is not good for young people. Discuss.

- Is there a problem with bullying in schools?

- Should we reorganize the school calendar?

- It doesn't matter what culture you come from. Discuss.

- People watch too much TV. Discuss.

- Young people are obsessed with electronic computer games when they should be spending time in the fresh air. Discuss.

- Should women earn the same money as men?

- Should we experiment or test our cosmetics on animals?

- How can we protect young people from drugs and alcohol?

- Keeping a pet helps you stay happy (and avoid stress).

- People want everything now and get into debt. Discuss.

- Shopping has become a national pasttime. Discuss.

- Write an article for a young person's magazine to persuade young people to: eat healthily, clean their teeth regularly or walk their dog often.

Can you think of any more topics to discuss?

Sally Ann Jones, wife of Peter and mother of four children, trained as a teacher in the 70's and has since worked as an elementary school teacher and private tutor as well as a freelance artist and illustrator. She exhibits her paintings and has published several as greeting cards.

This book is part of a series of educational material she has written based on the needs of the children she tutors.

Her daughter, Amanda, obtained a BA (Hons) in English Language, Linguistics and Sociology at the University of Surrey. She has completed an MA.

This book is dedicated to all the children who have tested it with such success.

For practice in Creative and Information Writing techniques and for more tips on writing good English and hints on good spelling, punctuation and grammar see the other books in our series.

Made in the USA
Middletown, DE
23 September 2017